WENDY RED STAR

HER DREAMS ARE TRUE

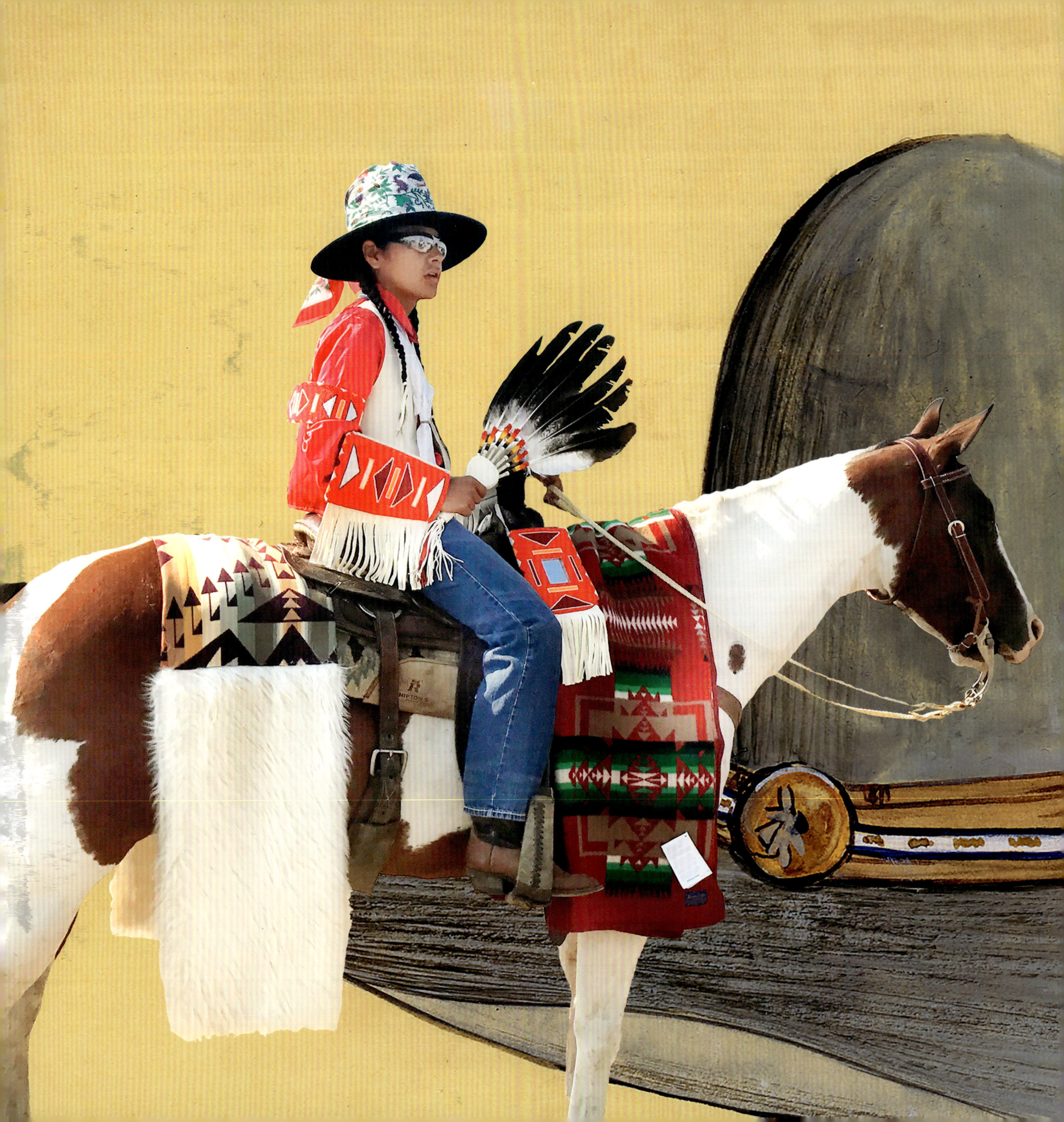

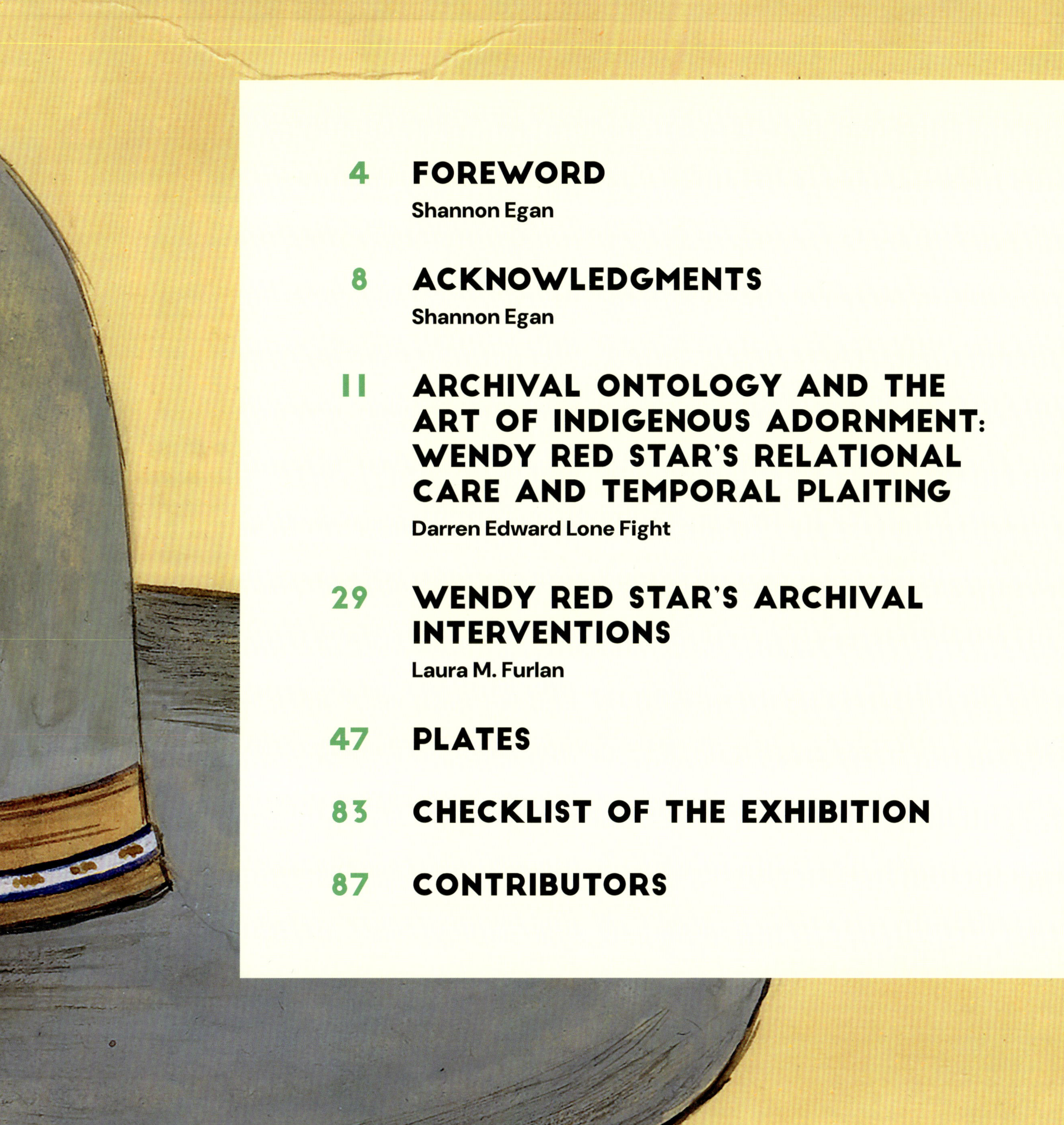

It's a thing that my grandpa and my dad would always say: if you put it in a book, then they think it's true. That statement is so accurate in terms of the writing about and cataloguing of Native objects. It's very rigid: this is what the object is, this is who the person is, this is what tribe they are, etc. Then you find out it's not that black and white.[1]

—Wendy Red Star

FOREWORD

SHANNON EGAN

The work of Apsáalooke artist Wendy Red Star is not black-and-white. Through the vivid colors of her photographs and prints that she refers to as her "Crow palette," Red Star disrupts ostensible truths and certainties typically sought by non-Native institutions when archiving Indigenous collections. Her vibrant works are on display in the exhibition at The Trout Gallery titled *Wendy Red Star: Her Dreams Are True*, which coincides with the presentation of Dickinson College's prestigious Arts Award to Red Star. As the first Indigenous artist to receive this award, Red Star is witness to a moment when the College is taking profound steps in reckoning with its past and present engagement with Indigenous peoples. In his essay that follows, Darren Edward Lone Fight articulates how the College's faculty and administration supported the Carlisle Indian Industrial School (CIIS) during its operation from 1879 to 1918. Situated less than two miles from Dickinson College in Carlisle, Pennsylvania, this institution served as the flagship off-reservation boarding school in the United States and was a central instrument in the federal government's policy of forced assimilation and cultural genocide of Indigenous peoples.[2] In Lone Fight's words, Red Star's work "strikes with visceral force in Carlisle, Pennsylvania." Photography was central to the visual propaganda of CIIS, and as Laura Furlan argues in this catalogue, Red Star's annotations on historical portraits and around images of Indigenous cultural belonging are "teaching us how to read these archival photographs, not through their original colonial framing, but through an Apsáalooke lens." Both Furlan and Lone Fight understand that Red Star's approach to archives and collections is both material and methodological. The artist's care in handling historical objects and photographs offers a new way of understanding these materials not as, in Lone Fight's words, "inert specimens trapped within anthropological taxonomies and institutional storerooms," but rather as an act of ongoing persistence, care, making, and revealing.

Ultimately, Red Star reclaims, reinterprets, and rematriates images and ideas, but her process is not simply revisionist. Cultural belongings and photographs are her media for expressing her own Apsáalooke identity as well as for empathizing with relatives who came to Carlisle. For example, Red Star explains:

I really identify with Alexander Upshaw [Apsáalooke/Crow, 1874 - 1909]. He was the interpreter for Edward S. Curtis [American, 1868-1952] when he came and photographed the Crow community in the early 1900s. The reason why I relate to him is he was in the first generation of Crow children who left the reservation and got an education. Granted, he had no choice. He went to the Carlisle Indian School. I just read some of his letters to the Carlisle newspaper. There's a ton of self-hatred in his letters about his identity during his time away from the reservation. And then he went through this transformation, where he came back to his culture and the reservation, and the local newspaper wrote about him—like, he went back to the blanket, which is what they would say about Native people who went back to their culture, back to being Apsáalooke. They went back to the blanket.[3]

Red Star suggests that Upshaw's story is not unambiguous; he was both a participant in assimilationist projects and an advocate for protecting the unity and conditions of the Crow Reservation.[4] Through his work with Curtis, as well as with photographers Frank Rinehart and Adolph Muhr, Upshaw can be seen, like Red Star, as an archivist-artist. And, because Upshaw and Red Star both left the Crow Reservation, their Indigenous identities are mutable and complex. Furlan's and Lone Fight's texts explain how Red Star's different series of prints and photographs may often center personal narratives, but they also question non-Native systems of cataloguing and create a new archive imbued with greater access and cultural meaning.

As seen in this catalogue and accompanying exhibition, several works from Red Star's *Apsáalooke Objects in Collections* series provide the viewer with detailed information about collections of cultural belongings and historical photographs, including names of depicted figures, personal observations, provenance, and dates. The works are documents of Red Star's research process and are organized around a single heritage object, such as a buckskin dress (fig. 1). With these carefully composed collages and handwritten notes, Red Star does not simply re-archive materials. Instead, each print serves as a kind of museum in itself—a didactic tool, a place for encountering the use, age, scale, provenance, and significance of her categories. Her new arrangements defy colonial modes of organization and reception. The annotations are reminders that photographs and objects are never silent; they signify stories beyond the metadata that a colonial institution includes in its database or wall label.

Red Star's creation of a new, Indigenous-focused archive responds to her observation that, "Since the time I left the Crow reservation I have encountered my tribe's material culture in every city I have exhibited or occupied. It is incredible that so much of my community's history and material culture is kept in the vaults of these institutions hundreds of miles away from their source."[5] The movement of significant belongings—often unwillingly by their makers and

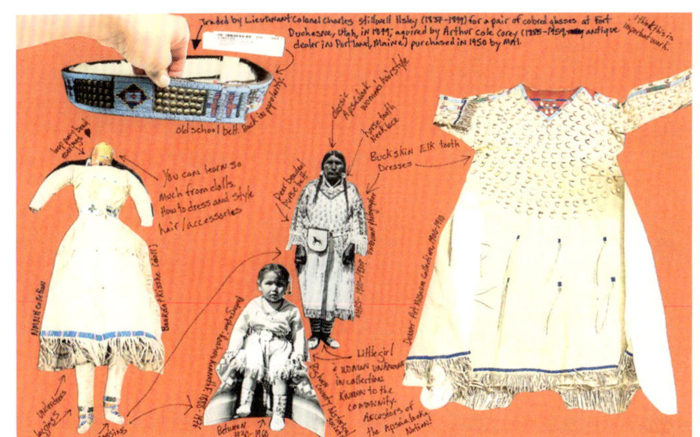

(**fig. 1**) Wendy Red Star (Apsáalooke (Crow), born 1981), *Set F: iíttaashteeuuxe (buckskin dress)*

2023

Archival pigment print on Satin Photo Rag, edition 3 of 3

16 x 25 in. (40.6 x 63.5 cm)

Purchase of the Friends of The Trout Gallery, 2025.19.2

Image courtesy of the artist and Sargent's Daughters © Wendy Red Star

Shannon Egan

communities—to institutions far away from their homes offers an uneasy parallel to the thousands of Indigenous children and young adults who were forcibly enrolled in off-reservation boarding schools, including CIIS. Red Star's *Apsáalooke* prints reunite belongings with others in the same family, alongside photographs of relatives. Although the objects may not have been de-accessioned (yet) from non-Native institutions, the collages stand in as imagined sites where dresses, belts, armbands, and bags, among other materials—each signifying the people who made, touched, and revered them—are welcomed home. In Red Star's hand, the motifs regain their personal and sacred meanings.

Some of the central themes in Red Star's work find precedents in previous exhibitions at The Trout Gallery that addressed the atrocities of CIIS, the resilience of its students, and a lasting archive of works by Indigenous artists. Beginning in 2004, Dickinson College students curated an exhibition titled *Visualizing a Mission: Artifacts and Imagery of the Carlisle Indian School 1879-1918*, and the exhibition *A Kiowa's Odyssey: A Sketchbook from Fort Marion* followed in 2007. Under the leadership of former Trout Gallery Director Phillip Earenfight, these exhibitions examined photographs from CIIS and ledger art by Etahdleuh Doanmoe (1856-1888), a member of the Kiowa Nation who made drawings about his experiences in captivity.[6] Concurrent exhibitions in 2018, *Re-Riding History and Shan Goshorn: Resisting the Mission*, featured work by contemporary artists in response to the archival materials housed in Carlisle. With profound personal connections to CIIS, Goshorn's exquisitely crafted baskets reflect her commitment to weaving past and present perspectives through photographs, family narratives, and institutional records as an act of resistance and persistence. With knowledge of this exhibition, Furlan rightly situates Red Star's work in relation to Goshorn's incorporation of Indigenous archives in her artistic practice. This network of connections continues, as Red Star credits Goshorn for encouraging her participation in the Smithsonian Artist Research Fellowship.[7]

With Lone Fight's discussion of how Red Star's archival practice confronts the institutional violence and photographic legacies of CIIS alongside Furlan's analysis of Red Star's process of "uncataloguing" materials from the grip of non-Native museums, this publication centers Red Star's perspective on Indigenous resistance and persistence. Taken together, Lone Fight and Furlan provide nuanced readings beyond the limited binaries of Indigenous and colonial, art and ethnography, as well as past and present. They articulate how Red Star's material practices and motifs—collage, annotation, and quilting, for example—can be used as metaphors for her aesthetic and conceptual strategies. Ultimately, Red Star's process is generative; she creates a new art-centered archive that engages with Indigenous sovereignty, survivance, and futurity.

The title of this exhibition catalogue is borrowed from Red Star's work featuring her great-great-grandmother, whose name in Apsáalooke translates to "Her Dreams Are True" (fig. 2). While this portrait honors an ancestral image, her poignant name also connotes both an insistent presentness and a radical alternative to non-Native frameworks of factuality.

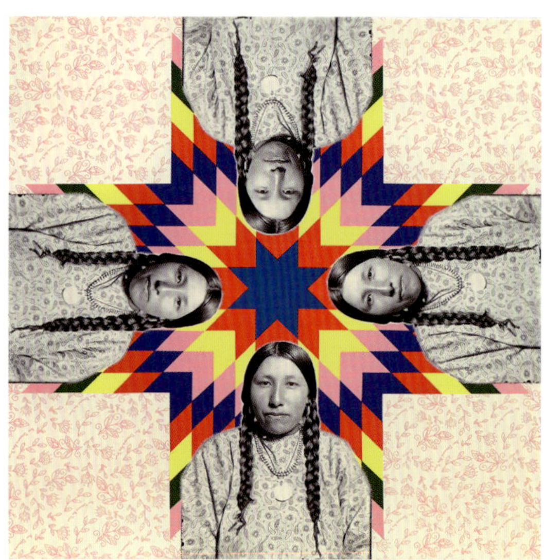

(fig. 2) Wendy Red Star (Apsáalooke (Crow), born 1981), *Her Dreams Are True (Julia Bad Boy)*

2021

Six-color lithograph on Somerset Satin soft white, with archival pigment printed chine collé on mulberry paper, edition 15 of 25

20.25 x 20 in. (51.4 x 50.8 cm)

Image courtesy of the artist and Sargent's Daughters © Wendy Red Star

In contrast to her grandfather's admonition to not believe books, or Western knowledge systems, simply as fact, her great-great-grandmother's name encourages a consideration of the true presence of different visions, the significance of ambitions, and the opportunity to create new realities. "Her Dreams Are True" may not be Red Star's namesake, but we see the family resemblance.

NOTES

1   Wendy Red Star, "Conversation, Annika Johnson," *Bíilukaa* (Radius Books, 2023), 183.

2   See Jacqueline Fear-Segal and Susan D. Rose, eds., *Carlisle Indian Industrial School: Indigenous Histories, Memories, and Reclamations* (University of Nebraska Press, 2016); Darren Lone Fight, "Archival Ontology and the Art of Indigenous Adornment: Wendy Red Star's Relational Care and Temporal Plaiting," in this volume.

3   Wendy Red Star, "Back to the Blanket: Wendy Red Star in Conversation with Josh T. Franco," *Wendy Red Star: Delegation* (Aperture, 2022), 34.

4   See Shamoon Zamir, *The Gift of the Face: Portraiture and Time in Edward S. Curtis's The North American Indian* (University of North Carolina Press, 2014); Wendy Red Star and Shannon Vittoria, "Apsáalooke Bacheeítuuk in Washington, DC: A Case Study in Re-Reading Nineteenth-Century Delegation Photography," *Panorama: Journal of the Association of Historians of American Art* 6, no. 2 (Fall 2020), https://doi.org/10.24926/24716839 .10672.

5   Wendy Red Star, *Bíiluka*, 11.

6   Molly Faust, Stephanie Latini, Kathleeen McWeeney, Kathryn M. Moyer, Laura Turner, Antonia Valdes-Dapena, *Visualixing a Mission: Artifacts and Imagery of the Carlisle Indian School, 1879–1918* (The Trout Gallery, 2004); Phillip Earenfight, ed., *A Kiowa's Odyssey: A Sketchbook from Fort Marion* (The Trout Gallery, 2007). Defined in the literature as "ledger art," Etahdleuh Doanmoe's drawings were assembled in an album titled *A Kiowa's Odyssey*, by Lieutenant Richard Henry Pratt, the founder of Carlisle Indian Industrial School. Typically associated with Plains Indians, ledger drawings were made first in the 1860s by Indigenous peoples using materials, such as accounting books, discarded by white settlers, military, and prison staff. See Janet Catherine Berlo, ed., *Plains Indian Drawings, 1865–1935: Pages from a Visual History* (Harry N. Abrams and the American Federation of Arts, 1996).

7   Phillip Earenfight, ed., *Re-Riding History: From the Southern Plains to the Matanzas Bay* (The Trout Gallery, 2018); Phillip Earenfight, ed., *Shan Goshorn: Resisting the Mission* (The Trout Gallery, 2018). On Red Star's acknowledgment of Shan Goshorn, see Red Star, "Back to the Blanket," 34.

Shannon Egan

Wendy Red Star: Her Dreams Are True is the result of much collaboration, generosity, and shared vision to make the exhibition, presentation at Dickinson College, and publication a reality. First, on behalf of The Trout Gallery and the Department of Art and Art History at Dickinson College, I thank Wendy Red Star for accepting the Dickinson College Arts Award. We are grateful for her insightful reflections on archival practices and her commitment to expanding knowledge about Apsáalooke culture.

ACKNOWLEDGMENTS

The Arts Award was initiated by Dickinson faculty who wanted to recognize and celebrate the achievements of individuals or groups that have made an outstanding contribution to the creative or performing arts. The Award was endowed in 1959 by gifts from the members of the Board of Trustees in honor of William W. Edel, president of Dickinson from 1946 to 1959. I thank Dickinson College President John E. Jones, III for presenting the award, and the faculty and staff of the Department of Art and Art History for initiating the invitation, coordinating the Arts Award Ceremony and hosting the artist's visit. Leading this effort are Elizabeth Lee and Melinda Schlitt, along with Todd Arsenault, Andy Bale, Anthony Cervino, Rachel Eng, Michele Karper, Jennifer Kniesch, Emily Lehman, and Ty Vanover.

In welcoming Red Star to campus, I am indebted to Amanda Cheromiah (Laguna Pueblo), Executive Director for the Center of the Futures of Native Peoples (CFNP); Jim Gerenscer, Director of the Carlisle Indian School Digital Resource Center (CISDRC) and Associate Dean for Archives and Special Collections; and Darren Lone Fight, Proud Member, Three Affiliated Tribes; Citizen of Mvskoke Nation and Assistant Professor, Department of American Studies. Their breadth and depth of knowledge and dedication to complicating and sharing the narratives and histories of the Carlisle Indian Industrial School are invaluable to me, along with their kind collegiality, good humor, and generous spirit. My admiration of Red Star's work is enhanced by their steadfast efforts to promote the study of North American Indigeneity at Dickinson College. As Lone Fight writes in his essay in this catalogue, "Like Red Star's careful handling of ancestral photographs, Cheromiah approaches the difficult archive of Carlisle with the same sacred attention: honoring the children who suffered while refusing to let their stories end in tragedy, transforming historical wounds into sites of healing and possibility." In addition to offering a powerful essay on Red Star and situating her work in Carlisle, Lone Fight initiated my introduction to Laura Furlan, Associate Professor of English at University of Massachusetts Amherst. As a result of Lone Fight's efforts serving as Founding Executive

Director of CFNP, I heard Furlan's engaging presentation on Red Star's work at the Central Pennsylvania Native American and Indigenous Studies Symposium at Dickinson College in 2024. I am thrilled that her contribution to this catalogue provides a comprehensive and nuanced analysis of the role of the archives across several series in the artist's oeuvre. Furlan and Lone Fight both have been wonderful collaborators through the process of creating this publication.

This exhibition would not have been possible without Christine Nyce, Sofia Love, and Allegra LaViola at Sargent's Daughters, who played fundamental roles in generously facilitating the loans, gracefully responded to myriad requests, and served as an essential conduit to Red Star. We are truly appreciative of Madalyn Barelle, Collections Manager, Archivist, and Studio Coordinator for Wendy Red Star Studio, for helping to coordinate Red Star's visit to Carlisle. I am grateful to Candice Hopkins and Amelia Russo at Forge Project for generously lending two works for this exhibition. Additional thanks to the Denver Art Museum, Denver Public Library, Cumberland County Historical Society, and artist Hulleah J. Tsinhnahjinnie for granting permissions, supplying images, and supporting research for this publication. I also sincerely appreciate Thomas Evans at Editorial Director of Artbook | D.A.P. for creating a wider readership for this publication.

At The Trout Gallery, I am lucky to work with an amazing team, including James Bowman, Collections Manager and Exhibition Designer, who beautifully designed this exhibition. In addition to her many impressive accomplishments developing creative educational programs, Heather Flaherty, Curator of Education also leads our beloved team of Trout Gallery student interns. We are thrilled that Post-Baccalaureate Fellow in Museum Education, Maddy Hull '24, Trout Gallery volunteer Hanna Alwine, and Summer Interns Reed Stone '26 and Georgia Mantione '26 researched Red Star, developed curricula for schools, and created materials for extensive educational outreach. Jen Marsh, Administrative Assistant for The Trout Gallery, attends to all details, large and small, and we all feel lucky to work with her. I am glad that our museum visitors are always warmly welcomed by Jolene Gregor, and Sue Russell. Finally, I have much appreciation for Ayumi Yasuda's exquisite graphic design.

Wendy Red Star: Her Dreams Are True was produced in part through the generous support of the Helen Trout Memorial Fund and the Ruth Trout Endowment at Dickinson College. Educational Programming is supported in part by The Trout Gallery Mumper-Stuart Educational Center.

Shannon Egan
Director, The Trout Gallery

ARCHIVAL ONTOLOGY AND THE ART OF INDIGENOUS ADORNMENT:

WENDY RED STAR'S RELATIONAL CARE AND TEMPORAL PLAITING

DARREN EDWARD LONE FIGHT

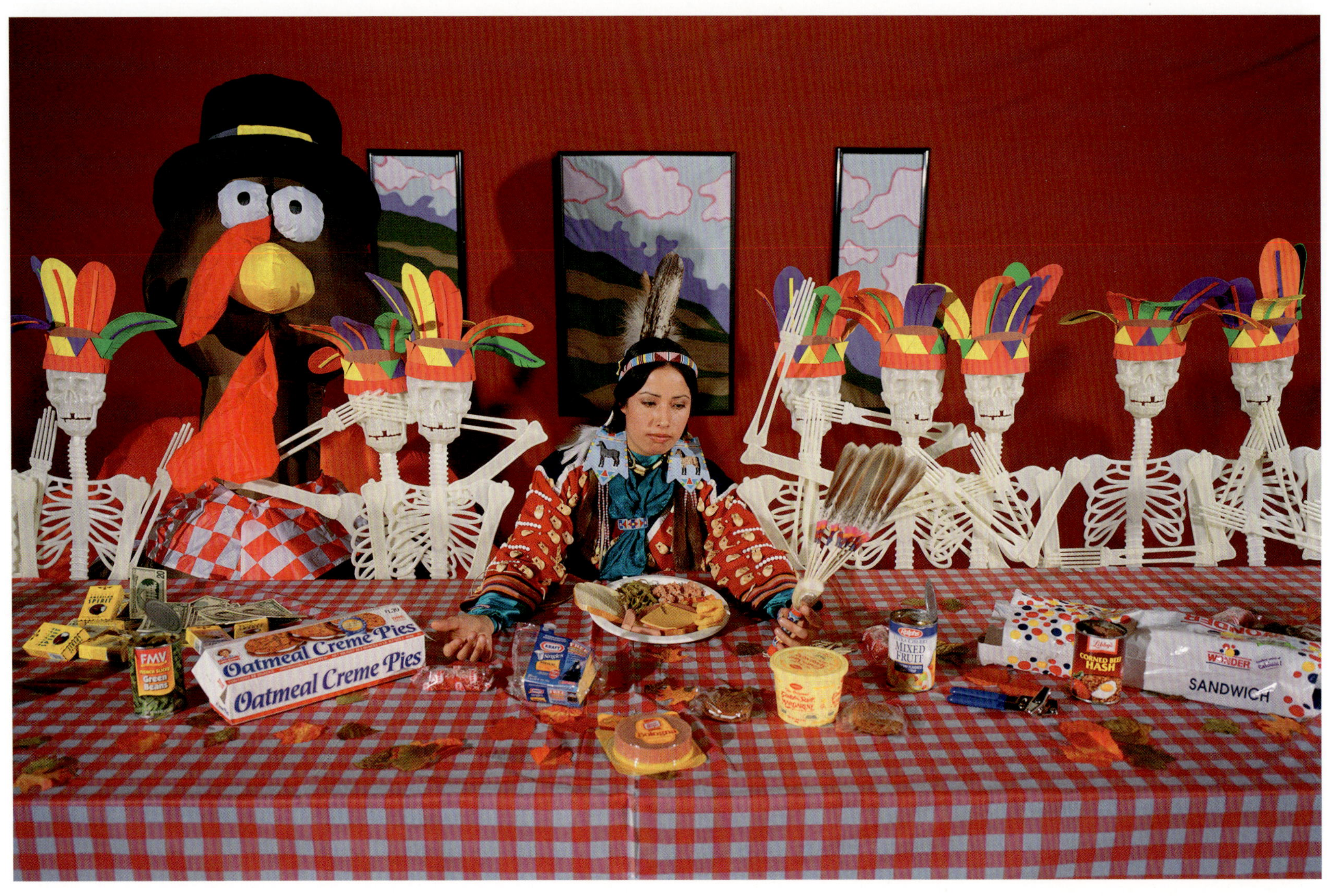

(fig. 1) Wendy Red Star (Apsáalooke (Crow), born 1981), *The Last Thanks*

2006

Archival pigment print

24 x 36 in. (61 x 91.4 cm)

Forge Project Collection, traditional lands of the Moh–He–Con–Nuck

Image courtesy of the artist and Sargent's Daughters © Wendy Red Star

Darren Lone Fight

ARCHIVAL ONTOLOGY AND THE ART OF INDIGENOUS ADORNMENT: WENDY RED STAR'S RELATIONAL CARE AND TEMPORAL PLAITING

DARREN EDWARD LONE FIGHT

Something is wrong with *The Last Thanks* (2006) (fig. 1). Wendy Red Star's (Apsáalooke Nation) meticulously constructed photograph presents an unsettling Thanksgiving tableau: plastic skeletons wearing flimsy paper headdresses flank Red Star, who sits centered and serene at a table in Apsáalooke regalia amid a calculated spread of foods, cigarettes, cash, and artificial décor.[1] The composition deliberately evokes a well-known painting while orchestrating a comedic assault on America's founding mythologies, transforming holiday nostalgia into a space of reckoning.[2] Red Star crystallizes this temporal collision elegantly, noting, "The first Thanksgiving is our last supper," a statement that reverberates through every element of her carefully orchestrated scene.[3] Harmonic tensions emerge as we notice Red Star's embodied Indigenous presence alongside the American Spirit cigarette packaging; these visual motifs share cultural intonation yet play in vastly different keys—one resonating with living ancestral knowledge, the other with plasticized commodified stereotypes. The color palette conducts a visual symphony dominated by yellows and reds with punctuating greens and blues, creating contrapuntal relationships between Red Star and the mass-produced holiday detritus: the Halloween-style skeletons providing macabre percussion against the overblown turkey's bombastic presence. These juxtapositions crescendo in the checked tablecloth pattern that visually samples, yet deliberately refuse harmonization with, the meticulous arrangement of elk teeth adorning Red Star's dress. This material dissonance generates both cultural critique and a knowing form of "NDN" humor: a complex composition where Indigenous presence refuses relegation to the background notes of America's self-congratulatory anthem.[4]

By positioning herself within the scene as both centerpiece and potential consumable, Red Star embodies the tension between cultural presence and cultural containment. The collision between authenticity and artifice vibrates through the composition, underscoring Red Star's larger project of exposing how Indigenous peoples have been staged, cataloged, or even taxidermied into settler historical narratives. This strategic self-positioning transforms what might otherwise be a simple parody into a profound ontological intervention. Red Star's living body disrupts the settler-colonial gaze by refusing both disappearance and static representation; instead, she occupies the ceremonial center with deliberate presence, her traditional regalia not a costume but a declaration of cultural continuity. The plastic skeletons with their paper headdresses serve as both foils and commentary, hollow representations of the "vanishing Indian" trope that haunts American cultural imagination. By placing herself at the center, alive, solemn, and unflinching, she reclaims the visual field, an act of sovereignty that insists upon the living continuity of Indigenous presence, even in a space overrun by the plastic monuments of settler mythmaking.

Through this embodied performance, Red Star challenges not just representations of Indigenous peoples but the very frameworks through which cultural memory is constructed and maintained. This juxtaposition illuminates a profound ontological and epistemological schism between Indigenous and Western approaches to cultural memory, i.e., the nature and being of objects and their relation to memory that operate from dramatically different traditions. Where Western ontological and epistemological systems conceptualize photographs and artifacts as inert objects requiring preservation through isolation behind glass to be only learned *about*, Indigenous ontologies often recognize these same items as animate participants in ongoing relational networks, demanding continued engagement and care to learn *alongside*.[5] If the settler archive functions as a mausoleum where cultural expressions are embalmed in permanent past tense, then Indigenous memory practices understand cultural materials as living entities requiring feeding and incorporation into community life. This fundamental difference stems from contrasting cultural traditions: Western thought, rooted in Enlightenment materialism, insists upon rigid boundaries between subject/object and past/present; many Indigenous worldviews recognize the permeable nature of these supposed binaries, understanding that "historical" objects continue to exert agency in the ongoing present and are not as far away as our references to or treatment of them might make us think.

Red Star's deliberate staging in *The Last Thanks* embodies this ontological critique with devastating precision while simultaneously enacting what Anishinaabe scholar Gerald Vizenor terms "survivance," an active presence that refuses victimry while asserting creative continuance and sovereign resistance.[6] Her living body, centered amid plastic artifacts and the "dead Indians" of settler mythology adorned in their performative grade–school headdresses, creates a specifically Indigenous comedic register through the deadpan juxtaposition of sacred and profane elements. This knowing humor operates beyond simplistic binaries of resistance/assimilation to establish what Vizenor calls a "postindian" consciousness that both acknowledges and moves beyond the simulations of "Indianness" that populate the American imaginary, even as it confronts narratives of displacement and dispossession. The ability to laugh at the absurdity of American historical narratives becomes itself an act of sovereign continuation, a refusal to be confined to the settler timeframe where we exist only in a permanent, taxidermied past.

The exhibition bears enormous weight in Carlisle, Pennsylvania, where Red Star's work now appears at The Trout Gallery. This place is less than two miles from the former Carlisle Indian Industrial School, to which Dickinson College gave material support in numerous ways.[7] This reprogramming camp operated from 1879 to 1918 with the implicit motto "Kill the Indian, Save the Man," and Red Star's investigations into archival representation confront this specific type of historical and institutional violence.[8] At Carlisle, photography was weaponized as propaganda; students were systematically photographed upon arrival and again after months of transformation, creating "before and after" image pairs that circulated to justify the school's assimilation program to the American public.[9] These institutional documents hauntingly echo the historical photographs that Red Star later annotates in her *Delegation* series, creating a sobering temporal continuity. Yet Red Star's artistic practice does not merely critique this visual violence. Her work transforms the very nature of how we understand archives, not as static repositories of the past, but as living spaces requiring care, adornment, and ceremonial tending in ways that echo how material objects function within Indigenous worldviews.[10]

This essay explores Red Star's artistic interventions in colonial archives as expressions of Indigenous adornment: a practice of relational care that extends meaning, encodes history, and honors what is significant in alignment with something interior to its essence. Indigenous adornment transcends mere decoration; it constitutes a reciprocal aesthetic act that restores proper relation between ancestral materials and contemporary communities

Darren Lone Fight

through intentional, material engagement. Through this framework, I offer interpretive motifs for Red Star's practice through two complementary modalities: beadwork and star-quilting. Like beadwork, her annotated photographs thread new strands of layered knowledge onto static records, building intricate networks of relation through accretive placement and meticulous attention to visual, textual, and cultural patterning. Like star-quilting, the patterned overlays in *Her Dreams Are True (Julia Bad Boy)* (Foreword, fig. 2) and others in this series piece together fragments of history, joining them into broader Indigenous aesthetic and cultural continuities through practices of ceremonial binding. While beadwork builds through textual and decorative accumulation, threading meaning bead-by-bead through carefully structured patterns of visual and conceptual relation, quilting creates through conjunction, binding elements into new constellations of belonging through the relational joining of edges that transform disparate elements into unified visual fields. Through these practices of Indigenous adornment, Red Star's work reconfigures the archive itself into a living space of transformation, relation, and care.

Adorning the Archive: Indigenous Aesthetics of Relational Care

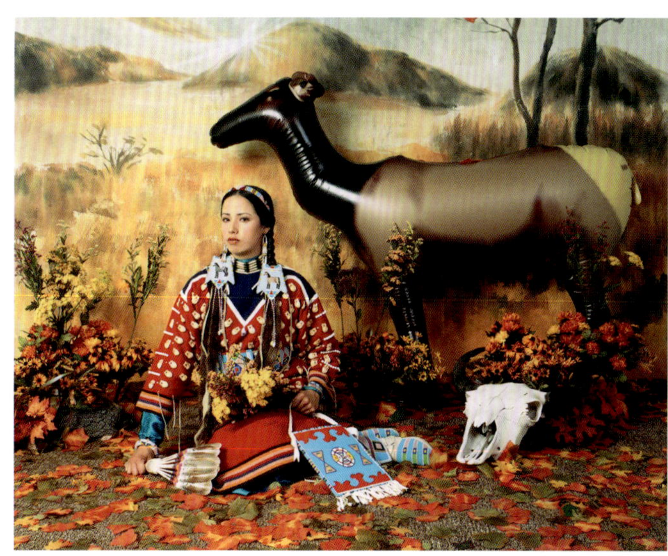

(fig. 2) Wendy Red Star (Apsáalooke (Crow), born 1981), *Four Seasons: Fall*
2006
Archival pigment print on photo paper
23 x 26 in. (58.4 x 66 cm)
Image courtesy of the artist and Sargent's Daughters © Wendy Red Star

Wendy Red Star's artistic trajectory can be traced from early, playful interrogations of settler-colonial imagery toward increasingly direct engagements with the archival-material base of that imaginary. Her early projects like *Interference* (2004)—a guerrilla installation of tipi frames across her undergraduate campus— and *Four Seasons* (2006), with its humorously incisive critique of ethnographic displays, demonstrate her core aesthetic strategies: layering, playful subversion of settler expectations, and provocative interactions with historical imaginaries. In *Four Seasons: Fall* (fig. 2), for instance, Red Star sits amid faux autumn foliage, polyester flowers, and an inflatable deer, its factory seams prominently displayed. This scene deliberately evokes the tradition of displaying Indigenous peoples in artificial "natural" settings that characterized early ethnographic exhibitions, where Native peoples were sometimes literally positioned within museum dioramas as living specimens.[11] The manufactured staging deliberately contradicts the romanticized "natural" settings of such displays, while Red Star's regalia and seemingly consternated expression assert her active existence against the taxidermic suspension commonly found in anthropological contexts. Even in these initial works, Red Star reveals the tensions between authenticity and artifice, truth, and performance, inviting viewers to recognize the living presence behind settler representations.

A notable shift in Red Star's oeuvre occurs with her landmark series, *1880 Crow Peace Delegation* (2014), which crystallizes her evolution from symbolically invoking settler-colonial archival practices to directly engaging with archival materials themselves.[12] In works like *Déaxitchish/Pretty Eagle* (fig. 3), she intervenes upon historical photographs with vibrant red ink annotations, transforming static ethnographic portraits into richly relational objects through meticulous cultural contextualization. Her annotations, a careful combination of explanatory text, directional indicators, and decorative elements, create multilayered fields of meaning that activate dormant cultural knowledge within these colonial records.

Vivid crimson ink creates striking visual contrast against the black-and-white photographs while simultaneously evoking the vermilion paint traditionally used in Crow ceremonial contexts, visually linking past and present through color symbolism. This approach transcends mere critique; she reclaims archival materials as living sites of Indigenous meaning-making. This shift from symbolic gestures toward actual relational acts of care, what I explore as forms of adornment, characterizes Red Star's trajectory as an artist and marks a distinctive contribution to contemporary Indigenous archival practices.

As Laura Furlan keenly observes in this catalogue through her analysis of Red Star's archival interventions, the artist "literally takes the archive into her own hands," transforming static historical materials into dynamic sites of Indigenous knowledge production.[13] This shared focus on Red Star's manipulation of archival materials reveals the complementary nature of our analyses; where Furlan emphasizes the political dimensions of Red Star's annotations, noting how they "highlight the absence of Apsáalooke context and knowledge in the photographs," my analysis extends this conversation by framing these interventions through Indigenous aesthetic practices of adornment: the red ink that both Furlan and I identify as central to Red Star's methodology functions simultaneously as political resistance and ceremonial care, a dual purpose that illuminates the inseparability of aesthetics and politics in Indigenous creative practice. By placing our analyses in conversation, we can appreciate how Red Star's work operates across multiple registers: as historical correction, cultural reclamation, and aesthetic innovation.

Red Star's practice emerges from a distinctly Indigenous understanding of archival materials as relational entities embedded in ongoing networks of ceremonial care and responsibility. Through increasingly confident adornment of colonial archives, Red Star transforms them from static repositories into vibrant relational spaces. Her interventions function as a counter-archive, re-centering Indigenous voices and aesthetics within colonial records. In *Peelatchiwaaxpáash/Medicine Crow* (fig. 4), Red Star uses red ink to trace the contours of the hair bow, brass rings, eagle feather fan, and ermine shirt and leggings, carefully outlining each item and explaining their significance. Her annotations reveal knowledge invisible within the original photograph: "Eagle feather fan [is a] symbol of leadership."[14] These simple notations perform complex cultural work, translating embodied knowledge into textual form while simultaneously asserting the living continuity of cultural practices represented in the image.

Through this process of annotation, Red Star engages in the reciprocity of adornment as a creative ethos. Adornment manifests here both materially and epistemologically as relational care and practice of mindful attention that honors what exists while extending its meaning through new layers of relation. Red Star's meticulous highlighting performs this work through careful selection of what to transform through the movement of her pen: some marks coalesce into letters-become-words, others flower as decorative elements or wayfinding indicators, but all build larger narrative patterns from scattered fragments, threading them together through context and care. The process mirrors Apsáalooke beadwork, where each individual bead carries meaning only when properly situated within the larger design. Red Star's annotations trace the contours of this meaning in her relatives' attire, the outlines bearing striking resemblance to beaded colorwork, while her explanatory notes carefully

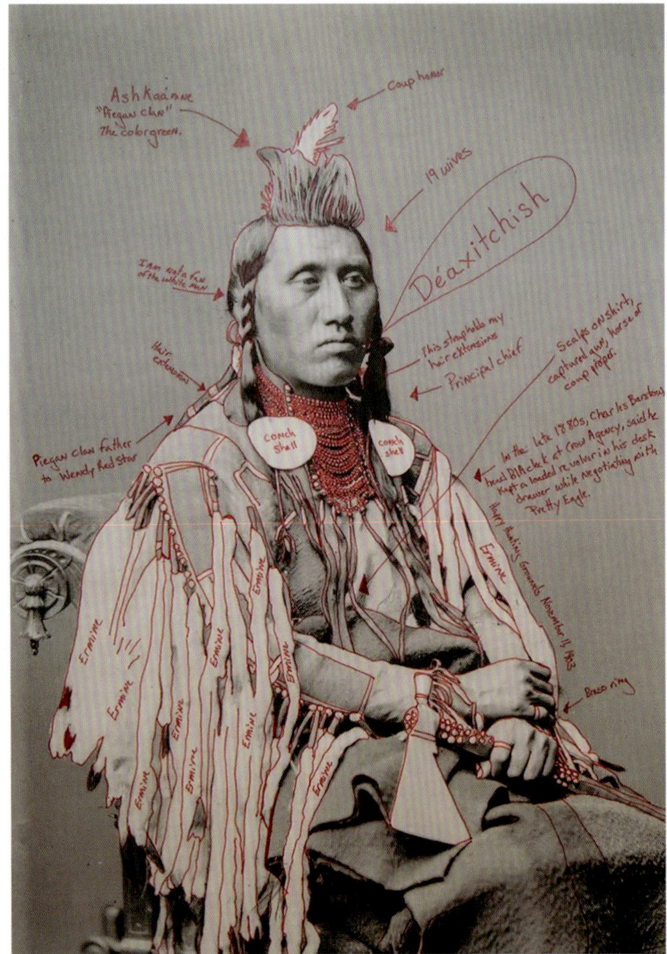

(fig. 3) Wendy Red Star (Apsáalooke (Crow), born 1981), *Déaxitchish / Pretty Eagle*

2014

Artist-manipulated digitally reproduced photograph by C.M. (Charles Milton) Bell, National Anthropological Archives, Smithsonian Institution

25 x 17 in. (63.5 x 43.2 cm)

Image courtesy of the artist and Sargent's Daughters © Wendy Red Star

contextualize the rich symbolism embedded in each element. The visual tension between her red ink tracings and the unrepresented colors they reference creates a layered perception, asking viewers to perceive the vivid cultural presence pulsing beyond the monochromatic constraints of nineteenth-century photography.

Red Star's approach must be understood against the contrast between Indigenous and Western knowledge traditions. Western archives, born of colonial impulses, often treat knowledge as a commodity, historical data to be collected, categorized, and controlled. In this paradigm, archives became tools of empire: repositories of artifacts and images gathered for study or domination, frequently divorced from their living contexts. Indeed, anthropological photography coincided with colonial expansion, producing images of Native peoples that served colonial narratives. Art Historian Jolene Rickard (Tuscarora Nation) notes that early photography emerged "at precisely the same moment" as the nineteenth-century expansion of U.S. takeover of Native lands, creating a powerful but distorted image of "the Indian" in the American imagination.[15] In Western archives, such photographs and records often remain indexed by museum catalog numbers or ethnographic labels, detached from the communities and stories they represent.

In more recent works, Red Star has shifted to symbolic interventions using visual motifs from Crow material culture. Her series *Crow's Shadow* (2021) consists of prints that overlay historic photographs of her Crow relatives with star quilt patterns in vibrant colors. In *Her Dreams Are True (Julia Bad Boy)* (Plate, p. 67), the eight-point star design, rendered in saturated hues of blue, red, yellow, pink, and purple, creates the background for a black-and-white portrait of her great-great grandmother, Julia Bad Boy.[16] The star appears to emanate from behind the photograph, as if emerging from another dimension: the ancestral world made manifest through color and pattern. Because the portrait repeats four times, Julia Bad Boy becomes the patterned star herself. One form does not merely frame the other, but creates a dynamic, cohesive, symmetrical whole with a sense of balance and centeredness while hailing the four directions. The organized patterning of the quilted star allows the original photograph to be clearly organized within the visual field while simultaneously transforming it, creating a layered composition that collapses distinctions between past and present. The floral motif in the four corners of the composition echoes the paisley design of Julia's dress, further connecting the portrait with the patterns and drawing the viewer's attention to her direct gaze, while the radiating points suggest connections beyond the frame. This powerful emblem of honor and care in Plains cultures envelops the ancestor's image in a gesture of ceremonial protection and recognition.

As Red Star explains, star quilts represent "something that people really treasure and hold onto" in Crow communities.[17] By merging this imagery with archival photographs, she performs a kind of visual giveaway: symbolically wrapping her ancestors in a star quilt, ceremonially honoring these individuals as beloved community members rather than anonymous "specimens" in museum collections. Her own great-great grandmother becomes part of this broad, spectral community, important individually but also made whole through communal affiliation and identification. This visual braiding of the individual and collective creates an elegant knotting that refuses the abstractive tendencies of settler archival practices which so often isolate Indigenous peoples from their relational contexts

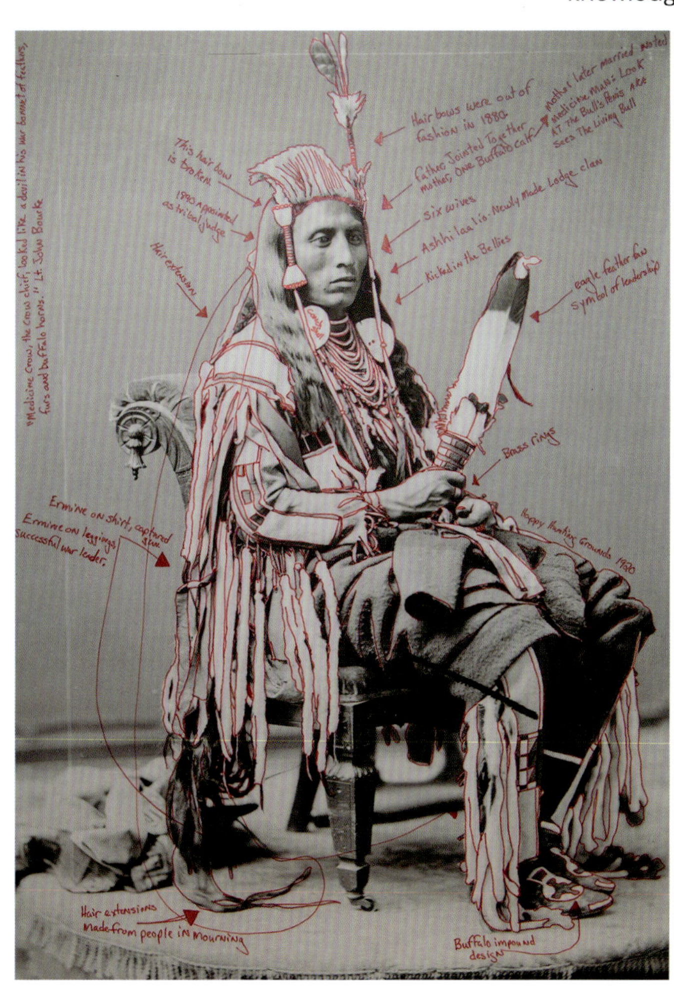

(fig. 4) Wendy Red Star
(Apsáalooke (Crow), born 1981),
Peelatchiwaaxpáash / Medicine Crow (Raven)

2014

Artist-manipulated digitally reproduced photograph by C.M. (Charles Milton) Bell, National Anthropological Archives, Smithsonian Institution

25 × 17 in. (63.5 × 43.2 cm)

Image courtesy of the artist and Sargent's Daughters © Wendy Red Star

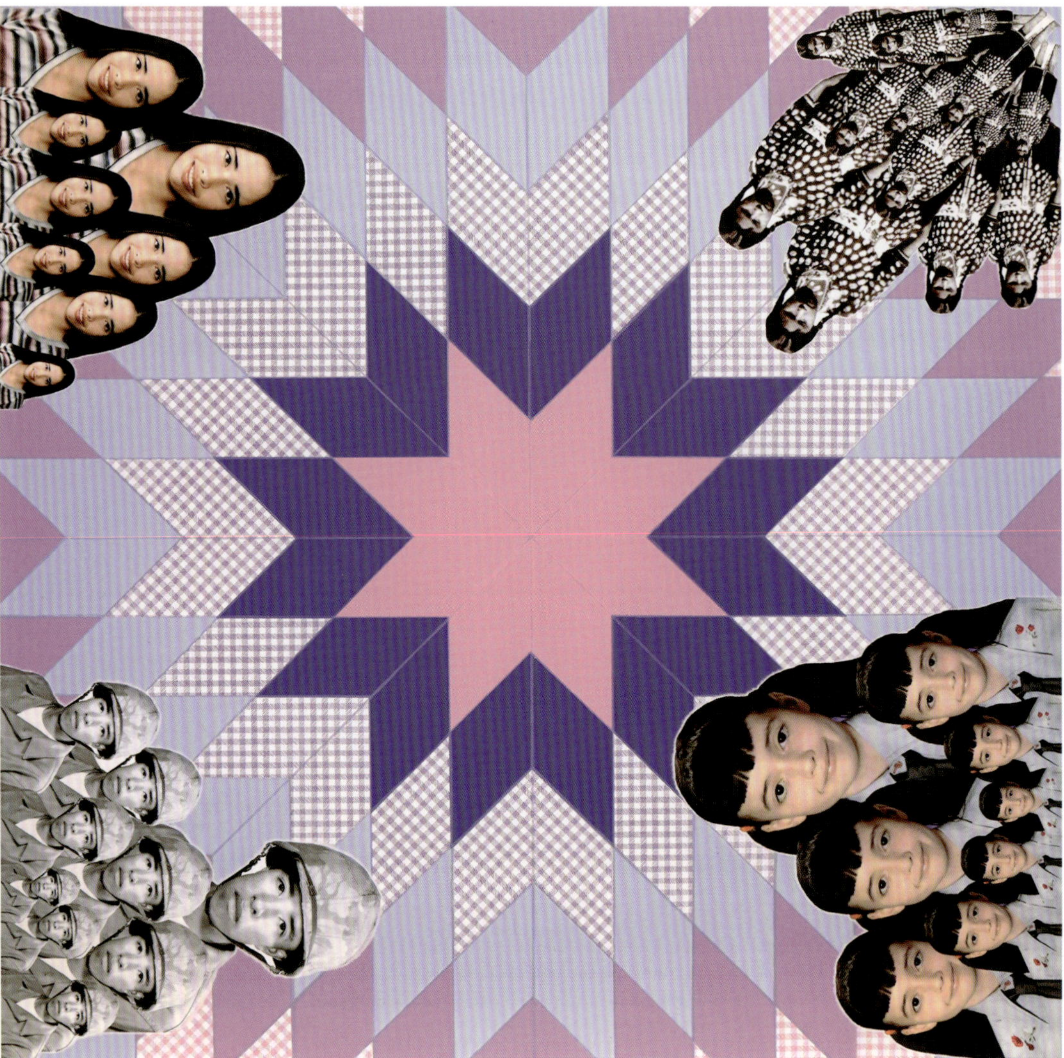

(fig. 5) Wendy Red Star (Apsáalooke (Crow), born 1981), *Four Generations*

2021

Six-color lithograph on Somerset Satin white, with archival pigment printed chine collé on mulberry paper, edition 15 of 16

30.25 x 30 in. (76.8 x 76.2 cm)

Image courtesy of the artist and Sargent's Daughters © Wendy Red Star

and render them as static objects of ethnographic curiosity. The geometric precision of the star pattern contrasts with the photographic grain of the archival image, creating a visual dialogue between different systems of representation—Western mechanical reproduction and Indigenous geometric abstraction—that suggests alternative ways of knowing and remembering. This juxtaposition does not simply place two visual regimes in conversation; it creates what I have termed in my work Oorútixubaa, a sacred knotting or imbricative attachment.[18]

The materiality and technique of her *Crow's Shadows* prints further illuminates this approach. Created through a meticulous, time-intensive process employing multi-color lithography on Somerset Satin paper fused with archival pigment-printed *chine collé* on mulberry paper, Red Star's technical complexity mirrors the layered attentiveness characteristic of adornment practices and manifests an Indigenous methodology where process embodies meaning. Each print requires multiple runs through the press, with separate plates for each color and precise registration to maintain the integrity of the pattern. The *chine collé* technique involves adhering gossamer mulberry paper to a stronger backing during the printing process, creating subtle textural variations within the finished piece. This physical stratification through different papers, inks, and impressions layered upon each other echoes the conceptual layering at work in Red Star's approach to archives. The careful physical layering of media becomes a tangible parallel to the conceptual layering of familial narratives, historical significance, and cultural meanings that coexist within a single frame, creating a textural topography within the print, inviting both visual and tactile engagement.

Red Star's engagement with quilting transcends conventional boundaries between medium and metaphor, embodying what we might consider a textile cosmology, a way of knowing and being that emerges through the deliberate interlacing of materials, memories, and meanings. Throughout her oeuvre, the star quilt operates not merely as an aesthetic element but as conceptual architecture, simultaneously structuring visual space and theoretical discourse. This patterned process serves as both container and activator for the archival fragments and lived narratives she brings into constellation. In *Four Generations* (fig.5), Red Star layers portraits of herself, her daughter, her father, and her grandmother against a vibrantly patterned star quilt that transcends decorative function to become an ontological field where relations are not merely represented but actively constituted. These star quilts are cherished ceremonial objects in Crow and other Indigenous communities that are often gifted at pivotal moments of celebration, ceremony, and/or transition. They also function as agential participants in the meaning-making process, their geometric rhythms, and adjoined-adornment orchestrating encounters between past, present, and emergent futures.

The distinctive eight-pointed star pattern, iconic within Indigenous quilting traditions across numerous nations, rises from a central nexus through meticulous construction: diamond-shaped fabric pieces cut and joined, expanding outward in concentric rings before tapering to precise points at the quilt's periphery. This radial geometry orchestrates a visual rhythm that carries the viewer's gaze through four generational portraits, refusing the linear progressive temporality of settler-colonial historical frameworks. Instead, the pattern insists on recursive, cyclical movements that echo Indigenous temporal understanding, ancestors and descendants existing in simultaneous relation, each calling the other into being. The star's form articulates a fundamental duality: rootedness concentrated in its central point, movement radiating through its eight arms. This geometric tension perfectly captures Indigenous identity as profoundly grounded in specific place while remaining dynamically responsive across time's fluid boundaries. Red Star positions ancestral and contemporary photographs within this pulsing pattern, awakening the quilt's ancestral purpose as story carrier, relation keeper, and ceremony of continuance. Through this placement, an ontological transformation unfolds: the colonial photographic archive, with its pretensions to capture and contain Indigenous life within static frames, becomes instead a breathing field of Indigenous becoming. The star's inexorable motion activates each image, allowing generations to touch one another through the fabric's sacred geometry.

Through these multivalent quilting practices, which operate simultaneously at material, symbolic, and epistemological levels, Red Star performs a profound transmutation of archival matter. She assembles dispersed fragments of memory, history, and identity into cohesive but non-homogenizing wholes that honor both the distinct nature of individual elements and their relational interdependence. The colonial photographs, once inert specimens trapped within anthropological taxonomies and institutional storerooms, undergo a metamorphosis into animate communicative entities that speak not only of what was but what continues to be and what might yet emerge. Their previously sterilized factuality—the presumed "objective" documentation that serves colonial knowledge systems—warms and quickens through embodied contextual reweaving into networks of familial affection, communal tradition, and living ceremony. The archive itself is thus reconceptualized: no longer a mausoleum housing the remains of supposedly "vanishing" peoples, it becomes instead a generative nexus of relation, its constituent elements vibrating with the frequencies of ongoing Indigenous presence, persistence, and futurity. The quilt, in Red Star's hands, becomes both method and theory, a way of making and knowing that challenges linear, extractive approaches to cultural heritage while modeling alternative possibilities for memory-work that sustains rather than suspends Indigenous lifeways.

This aesthetic praxis of Indigenous adornment illuminates interconnections across multiple modalities of Red Star's work, resonating with Laura Furlan's incisive observations about the artist's engagement with ethnographic refusal and archival rematriation. Furlan rightly notes that Red Star's interventions with archival materials "makes them accessible to a wider audience, at the same time it draws attention to the collections themselves—what has been preserved, by whom, and why—and what this says about the value of archives, Indigenous praxis, and ethnographic refusal."[19] This observation braids together seamlessly with my analysis of adornment as relational care that extends meaning rather than containing it: both perspectives recognize that Red Star's work transforms not merely individual archival objects but radically reconfigures the ontological status of the archive itself. While Furlan's political analysis and my framework of adornment as relational care illuminate comple-mentary dimensions of Red Star's practice, the implications extend beyond critique toward generative possibility. The beaded edges, quilted backgrounds, and annotative adornment thus inaugurate what we might call archival futurity: a methodology that transforms colonial records into sites where ancestral knowledge seeds contemporary and future Indigenous aesthetics, scholarship, and ceremony.

When considered within the broader landscape of Indigenous artists engaging with colonial archives—such as Hulleah Tsinhnahjinnie's (Diné [Navajo] Nation) photographic re-captions that restore agency to historical subjects, Catherine Blackburn's (English River Dene First Nation) beaded photographs that literally pierce the colonial image with Indigenous materiality, or Deborah Miranda's literary excavation of mission records in *Bad Indians* that transforms bureaucratic documentation into poetry of survivance—Red Star's work emerges as part of a constellation of practices reimagining archives not as repositories of the past but as generative sites of ongoing Indigenous sovereignty.[20] This collective reimagining suggests that the future of Indigenous archival engagement lies not in the sterile preservation of cultural fragments but in their ceremonial reincorporation into living networks of relation, where objects once cataloged as specimens can be reawakened as relatives deserving of care, conversation, and continued co-creation.

Red Star's distinctive contribution lies in her sophisticated deployment of these relational frameworks. By using beadwork's accumulative logic alongside quilting's connective symbolism she weaves together what settler conceptual schemas forcibly separate: craft and concept, art and scholarship, archive and ceremony, individual and collective memory. The adornment practices she employs constitute nothing less than an Indigenous theory of knowledge production, one that understands meaning-making as inherently material, relational, and ongoing rather than abstract, individualistic, and fixed. What emerges is a distinctly Indigenous aesthetic methodology that refuses binary oppositions (traditional/contemporary, artistic/scholarly, physical/digital, individual/collective) while performing vital acts of visual sovereignty that reclaim not only archival content but the very epistemological frameworks through which we encounter, understand, and relate to the past itself.[21] She does not merely show us different images but invites us to see differently, to participate in a visual field where adornment is not supplementary but centrally constitutive of meaning itself.

Reckoning and Resurgence: Dickinson, Carlisle, and Beyond

Red Star's *Her Dreams Are True* strikes with visceral force in Carlisle, Pennsylvania, where the historical violence of the former Carlisle Indian Industrial School (CIIS) continues to lacerate institutional and cultural memory. As noted above, photography at Carlisle functioned as a propagandistic tool, weaponized by the settler state to justify the attempted cultural genocide, with students systematically documented in "before and after" image pairs that circulated to amplify the school's assimilation program. These institutional compositions haunt Carlisle's historical memory in ways resonant with the archival photographs Red Star annotates in her exhibited works, creating a temporal collision across centuries.

In this charged landscape, Red Star's interventions in archival photographs directly confront institutional violence through deliberate transformations: vivid annotations, star quilt patterns, and repurposed catalog numbers refuse the notion of archival objects as silent historical artifacts. Instead, they become living documents animated by contemporary Indigenous perspectives and knowledge systems. By foregrounding names, histories, and ceremonial aesthetics deliberately muted by colonial photographers and bureaucrats, Red Star creates works that amplify Indigenous presence rather than relegating it to background notes, itself a powerful counterpoint to the institutional narratives that once defined this place. Though Red Star works with archival materials distinct from those generated by CIIS, her methodologies offer profound insights into how Indigenous artists can transform static archives beyond mere scholarly repositories into sites of living engagement and cultural reclamation.

Carlisle's institutional landscape carries the weight of entangled histories, not the least of which is Dickinson College's deep imbrication with the Carlisle Indian Industrial School. Faculty members doubled as CIIS chaplains and instructors; for instance, Professor Joshua Lippincott, class of 1858, delivered sermons that sanctified the assimilationist doctrine while Professor Charles Francis Himes, class of 1855, regularly shuttled between campuses, giving lectures that lent academic authority to cultural genocide.[22] Dickinson President James Andrew McCauley assisted on the Board of Trustees of the Carlisle Indian School Charity Fund, facilitating land transactions that expanded the school's territorial reach, signing contracts for the Hocker Farm between 1883–1889, giving the first sermon in the newly built chapel, and attending CIIS commencements where he lent institutional gravitas to ceremonies that celebrated the systematic destruction of Indigenous identity.[23] This collaboration reveals how academic institutions, cloaked in educational benevolence, became active instruments in the federal machinery of forced assimilation. The proximity was not merely geographic but ideological: two institutions separated by mere miles, united in their so-called civilizing missions. The violence was not merely adjacent but constitutive: knowledge production and cultural destruction operating as twin engines of the same colonial apparatus, each legitimizing the other through personnel, resources, and conviction.

This institutional complicity extends beyond historical entanglement into contemporary extraction. On September 17, 2004, Dickinson College converted colonial legacy into capital, selling 65.1 acres to Keystone Arms Associates for $1,850,000: land that traced its provenance to the CIIS. The property, originally conveyed to the United States/CIIS by Christopher G. Kritz and Anna E. Kritz in 1901 during a period when Dickinson College maintained active collaboration with CIIS through faculty chaplains, student volunteering services, and shared educational programming, was then transferred to Dickinson College via federal quitclaim deed dated December 18, 1961, for the princely sum of $1.[24] This transaction represents profit extracted from property that entered the boarding school system during Dickinson's ongoing institutional partnership with the CIIS, creating a loop wherein the college's entanglement with Indigenous erasure eventually yielded nearly two million dollars in profit. The college's ability to monetize this land four decades after receiving it from federal hands collapses any comfortable distance between historical injustice and present benefit. Here, the ongoing nature of settler colonialism reveals itself not through metaphor but through property law: institutions continuing to harvest value from lands saturated with Indigenous dispossession, each deed transfer extending the original violence into perpetuity.

Against this backdrop, the Carlisle Indian School Digital Resource Center (CISDRC) at Dickinson College represents a different approach to historical responsibility. For over a decade, CISDRC has undertaken the painstaking work of digital recovery, transforming thousands of pages and photographs from CIIS archives into accessible resources for descendants and scholars. Jim Gerencser, the current director of CISDRC and Associate Dean for Archives and Special Collections, Susan Rose, the former co-director and Professor of Sociology, and Barbara Landis, who served as the Carlisle Indian School biographer and historian at the Cumberland County Historical Society, have collectively labored to liberate these materials from institutional entombment. Landis's work began with a simple act of care: answering inquiries from descendants seeking traces of their relatives who vanished into the school's bureaucratic maw.[25] From this seed grew comprehensive student rosters and digital infrastructures under the careful guidance and sustained effort of Landis, Gerencser, and Rose, designed explicitly to return names to their nations, to restore kinship severed by administrative violence. Through ongoing partnerships with Indigenous communities, these archival fragments undergo transformation: revisions, annotations, and adornments convert them from static artifacts of imperial surveillance into living testimonies of survivance and continuity.

In 2020, I joined Dickinson College as its first Indigenous tenure-track faculty member, a particular kind of arrival given the institution's historical entanglements with the Carlisle Indian Industrial School, where many of my Three Affiliated Tribes (MHA) relatives were students. The weight of being in a place so suffused with important meaning meant carrying both possibility and memory through every classroom, event, and meeting. Nevertheless, this appointment opened a space for what would become the Center for the Futures of Native Peoples (CFNP), an interdisciplinary initiative started through vision documents, strategic planning, a partnership with the Mellon Foundation, and support from Dickinson's leadership, faculty, and staff. From initial concept to secured funding, the work of building CFNP became an act of reclamation: transforming institutional space into Indigenous place.

The center emerged from recognizing that Dickinson's proximity to this site of historical trauma demanded more than acknowledgment. It called for a fundamental reimagining of how Indigenous presence moves through this place where erasure was once federal policy.

The CFNP works in a vital relationship with our sister center, CISDRC, which undertakes the meticulous work of digitizing and providing access to the CIIS archives. Where CISDRC excavates and preserves, the CFNP builds forward: we take these recovered materials and connect them to contemporary Indigenous futures through programming that refuses to let history remain merely historical. Together, these centers work together, with CISDRC's archival recovery feeding the CFNP's mission of Indigenous resurgence and community engagement, transforming documents of attempted destruction into active sites of ongoing creation.

The CFNP has cultivated partnerships with tribal nations across the country, becoming particularly active in reshaping how Carlisle's history is understood and interpreted beyond the confines of tragic narrative. When the former CIIS grounds received designation as a national monument through Presidential declaration in 2024, Dickinson College committed to partnering with the federal government in the site's interpretation. This collaboration promises new interpretive materials, educational programs, and commemorative events that emphasize Indigenous resilience, survivance, and contemporary presence rather than rehearsing narratives of disappearance. Dr. Amanda Cheromiah (Laguna Pueblo), who assumed the position of executive director of the CFNP in 2024, brings extraordinary depth to this work through her scholarly expertise in Indigenous education and communi-ty-engaged research. As a descendant of six grandparents who survived the Carlisle Indian Industrial School, her leadership shoulders both personal and intellectual weight, transforming generational memory into purposeful and meaningful action. Under her guidance, the center has flourished through innovative programming that weaves together archival recovery with contemporary cultural revitalization, while she simultaneously undertakes the vital, often unrecognized labor of creating a physical space of care and comfort for Indigenous peoples visiting Carlisle. Her vision transforms what was once a site of institutional violence into a place of gathering, rest, and renewal, establishing the CFNP as both an intellectual hub and a cultural sanctuary. This multifaceted approach embodies the center's mission: not merely to document historical trauma but to actively nurture Indigenous futures through scholarship, ceremony, and community. Like Red Star's careful handling of ancestral photographs, Cheromiah approaches the difficult archive of Carlisle with sacred attention born of intimate knowledge: honoring our relatives while transforming historical wounds into sites of healing and possibility.

Additionally, and perhaps most significantly, Dickinson College, through the CISDRC and CFNP, has actively participated in the ongoing sacred work of facilitating the rematriation of students who died at the Carlisle Indian Industrial School back to their tribal communities. Since 2017, the U.S. Army, which oversees the former school grounds, has collaborated with tribal nations to disinter and rematriate these children with increasing care and frequency. Over 40 students' remains have journeyed home to their Peoples since the program began, with numbers growing significantly in 2024 and culminating in 19 children coming home in 2025, the largest group to date. The tribes leading these efforts include the Northern Arapaho, Rosebud Sioux, Oglala Lakota, Cheyenne and Arapaho Tribes of Oklahoma, Seminole Nation of Oklahoma, and Oneida Nation (who have reclaimed five of their relatives), among many others who continue this essential work of bringing their relatives home. CFNP and CISDRC support these sacred returns through meticulous research, careful documentation, and respectful public education, recognizing that each rematriation represents not merely the correction of historical wrong but the restoration of children to their rightful place within the ongoing ceremony of their Peoples' existence. These acts of return complete circles that colonial violence attempted to sever, reuniting children with the lands and ancestors who have been calling them home for over a century.

The college's ongoing response to the CIIS legacy thus transcends mere acknowledgment, embodying instead a sustained commitment to institutional transformation and ethical relationship–building that moves from recognition toward active partnership and material change. Within this evolving landscape, Red Star's presence at The Trout Gallery carries extraordinary weight. Her practice of archival adornment, threading new knowledge through static records, binding fragments into fresh constellations of belonging, creates a profound counterpoint to the institutional violence that once saturated this place. The meticulous beadwork of her annotations, the ceremonial patience of her quilted overlays, constitute visual sovereignty in action. These interventions do not simply speak back to colonial power; they fundamentally reconfigure the terrain of engagement, inscribing survivance into the archive's very structure.

By hosting *Her Dreams Are True*, The Trout Gallery enters this transformative current not as arbiter but as participant in collective reckoning. The exhibition makes no pretense of healing wounds that institutions like CIIS carved into Indigenous communities, nor does it position artistic intervention as sufficient response to historical violence's material consequences. What it creates instead is generative space: a convergence where different approaches to history, memory, and relation can meet and transform one another, where Indigenous perspectives command the center rather than haunting the margins, where the archive itself shifts from tomb to forum, hosting urgent conversations between ancestors and descendants, past violations and future possibilities.

Through her distinctive methodology, Red Star reveals archives as they truly are, not neutral repositories but active sites of power, memory, and potential transformation.[26] Her work demonstrates how colonial documentation can be ceremonially reclaimed, how records meant to catalog erasure can become grounds for resurgence. She does not merely annotate history; she opens portals through which new relationships with historical materials become possible, honoring their weight while activating their capacity for healing. Here in Carlisle— this ground where children's Indigenous languages bled into silence, where ancestral songs met federal prohibition, and sacred ceremonies were criminal acts—Red Star's visual interventions pulse with the power of resurgence. Their vibrant presence resonates long after gallery lights dim, opening not wounds but windows, offering not closure but continuance, asserting not tragedy but transformation: the persistent creative force of Indigenous life refusing every imposed impossibility.

1   Following increasingly common practice across academic journals, especially those in Native American and Indigenous Studies, I have not italicized Indigenous words. This typically marks them as foreign or otherwise estranged, which, in this context, they are obviously not. As seen in this work, the $20 bill lies face-down, Andrew Jackson's portrait buried beneath the feast—a deliberate interment of the architect of Indigenous removal. Paired with $2 bills bearing Jefferson's visage, this currency becomes a meditation on American tender: how founding fathers trafficked in both democratic ideals and human displacement, their faces now circulating as the very medium of exchange built upon dispossessed lands.

2   Red Star explicitly refers to Leonardo da Vinci, *The Last Supper*, 1498, tempera and oil on plaster, Santa Maria delle Grazie, Milan. Red Star's appropriation performs a double operation: reverence and rupture, homage and hijacking. As da Vinci's fresco dried on Milanese walls, Columbus was departing Spanish shores for his third voyage to the Caribbean. Two European ventures unfolded in parallel: one revealing divine order through Renaissance perspective, the other orchestrating Indigenous apocalypse through imperial conquest. Red Star collapses these temporal coordinates, making visible how Western civilization's highest cultural achievements and its most brutal extractions share the same historical breath, a simultaneity her work elegantly indexes.

3   Tiffany Midge, "The Last Thanks, 2006," *The Brooklyn Rail*, July/August 2023, https://brooklynrail.org/2023/07/1by1/The-Last-Thanks-2006/.

4   NDN humor refers to a distinct form of Indigenous comedy that often uses irony, satire, and/or cultural inside jokes to address colonial violence and stereotypes. This form of humor frequently juxtaposes sacred and profane elements and/or ironic engagement to highlight absurdities in settler-colonial narratives while affirming Indigenous resilience. See Vine Deloria Jr., "Indian Humor," in *Custer Died for Your Sins: An Indian Manifesto* (University of Oklahoma Press, 1988), 146-167; and Aitor Ibarrola-Armendariz, "Native American Humor as Resistance: Breaking Identity Moulds in Thomas King's *Green Grass, Running Water*," *Miscelánea: A Journal of English and American Studies* 42 (2010): 67-90. The term 'NDN' is a reclaimed shorthand for 'Indian' used by many Indigenous Peoples in contemporary discourse. E.g., Peters, Pamela J. "Real NDNZ." In *#NotYourPrincess: Voices of Native American Women*, ed. Lisa Charleyboy and Mary Beth Leatherdale (Annick Press, 2017), 68. This is a photographic work of resistance that recasts Hollywood icons with Indigenous actresses; the title employs "NDNZ" as reclaimed terminology.

5   For further discussion of Indigenous ontological approaches to material culture and archives, see Kimberly Christen, "Opening Archives: Respectful Repatriation," *The American Archivist* 74, no. 1 (Spring/Summer 2011): 185-210, which examines collaborative digital repatriation projects that recognize the animate nature of archival materials within Indigenous knowledge systems. Ruth B. Phillips, "Making Sense Out/Of the Visual: Aboriginal Presentations and Representations in Nineteenth-Century Canada," *Art History* 27, no. 4 (September 2004): 593-615, offers a complementary analysis of how Indigenous visual systems operate through relational networks of meaning that resist Western taxonomic containment. See also Jennifer R. O'Neal, "'The Right to Know': Decolonizing Native American Archives," *Journal of Western Archives* 6, no. 1 (2015): 1-17, which articulates Indigenous approaches to archival materials as living entities requiring ongoing ceremonial care; and, of course, Vine Deloria Jr., *God is Red: A Native View of Religion*, 30th Anniversary Edition (Fulcrum Publishing, 2003), 65-78.

6   Gerald Vizenor, *Manifest Manners: Narratives on Postindian Survivance* (University of Nebraska Press, 1994), 53.

7   For deeper scholarly analysis of the Carlisle Indian Industrial School and the broader boarding school system, see David Wallace Adams, *Education for Extinction: American Indians and the Boarding School Experience, 1875–1928* (University Press of Kansas, 1995), 52-57; and K. Tsianina Lomawaima, *They Called It Prairie Light: The Story of Chilocco Indian School* (University of Nebraska Press, 1994). Adams details how Carlisle served as the model for dozens of similar institutions across the United States, while Lomawaima examines how Indigenous students navigated and resisted these assimilationist structures.

8   This phrase is attributed to Richard Henry Pratt, founder of the Carlisle Indian Industrial School. While not his exact words, it summarizes his philosophy of forced assimilation. Pratt's actual statement was: "A great general has said that the only good Indian is a dead one... In a sense, I agree with the sentiment, but only in this: that all the Indian there is in the race should be dead. Kill the Indian in him, and save the man." See Richard Henry Pratt, *Battlefield and Classroom: Four Decades with the American Indian, 1867–1904*, ed. Robert M. Utley (University of Oklahoma Press, 2003), 335.

9   Pratt, 260-261. The photographic practices at Carlisle are extensively documented in Jacqueline Fear-Segal and Susan D. Rose, eds., *Carlisle Indian Industrial School: Indigenous Histories, Memories, and Reclamations* (University of Nebraska Press, 2016), especially 90-118, which analyzes how these "before and after" photographs functioned as visual propaganda for the assimilation project. See also Hayes Peter Mauro, *The Art of Americanization at the Carlisle Indian School* (University of New Mexico Press, 2011), 45-78, which examines how these photographs constructed racial hierarchies while simultaneously

providing spaces for Indigenous resistance. Linda F. Witmer, *The Indian Industrial School, Carlisle, Pennsylvania, 1879-1918* (Cumberland County Historical Society, 1993), 45-67, provides additional historical context for the school's photographic archive.

10   In her interview with Emily Moazami, Red Star discusses the importance of collaboration between communities and institutions in building connections that strengthen collective knowledge of archival materials, emphasizing how descendants play a crucial role in 'repersonalizing' historical photographs. See Wendy Red Star and Emily Moazami, "People of the Earth," in special issue, "Native America," *Aperture Magazine* 240 (Fall 2020): 45-52, https://aperture.org/interviews/people-of-the-earth-wendy-red-star/.

11   These ethnographic displays existed within a broader settler-colonial visual regime where Indigenous peoples were exhibited as living curiosities in "human zoos" and world's fairs. Buffalo Bill's "Wild West shows," while offering employment opportunities, simultaneously reinforced the "vanishing Indian" narrative by presenting Indigenous performers as noble but defeated relics of the past. Wendy Red Star directly engages with this complex legacy through works like the above referenced *Four Seasons* (2006), which brilliantly subvert these historical modes of display. For further reading, see: Robert W. Rydell, *All the World's a Fair: Visions of Empire at American International Expositions, 1876-1916* (University of Chicago Press, 1984); Richard Slotkin, "Buffalo Bill's 'Wild West' and the Mythologization of the American Empire," in *Cultures of United States Imperialism*, ed. Amy Kaplan and Donald E. Pease (Duke University Press, 1993), 164-181; and Emily C. Burns, *Transnational Frontiers: The American West in France* (University of Oklahoma Press, 2018).

12   Abaki Beck, "Decolonizing Photography: A Conversation with Wendy Red Star," *Aperture*, December 14, 2016, 37, https://aperture.org/editorial/wendy-red-star/.

13   Laura M. Furlan, "Wendy Red Star's Archival Interventions," in this volume.

14   Wendy Red Star and Shannon Vittoria, "Apsáalooke Bacheeítuuk in Washington, DC: A Case Study in Re-Reading Nineteenth-Century Delegation Photography," *Panorama: Journal of the Association of Historians of American Art* 8, no. 1 (Fall 2020): 12, https://journalpanorama.org/article/re-reading-american-photographs/apsaalooke-bacheeituuk-in-dc/.

15   Rickard notes that photography emerged as a technology concurrent with westward expansion and the dispossession of Native lands, creating a visual record that often served colonial narratives. See Jolene Rickard, "Sovereignty: A Line in the Sand," *Aperture* 139 (Summer 1995): 50-59.

16   Fred E. Miller, a Bureau of Indian Affairs clerk stationed at the Crow Agency in Montana from 1898 to 1910, produced a significant photographic record of Apsáalooke (Crow) life during a period of profound transformation. Miller, who was adopted into the Crow Nation, photographed Her Dreams Are True (Julia Bad Boy), the great-great grandmother of Red Star. For more on Miller's photography, see "Fred E. Miller Collection," National Museum of the American Indian, Smithsonian Institution, https://americanindian.si.edu/collections-search/edan-record/ead_collection%3Asova-nmai-ac-108.

17   Wendy Red Star and Emily Moazami, "People of the Earth."

18   Note that this is not a traditional community term of my Peoples, but a technical term developed in my scholarly work. I introduced this term in my dissertation, "Indigenous Impositions in Contemporary Culture: Knotting Ontologies, Beading Aesthetics, and Braiding Temporalities" (PhD diss., University of Massachusetts Amherst, 2021), 63-64: "Oorútixubaa, this articulated imbricative attachment, I derive from a Hiraacá illustration of the relationship between social and ceremonial organization and time. When attempting to explain to his consternated interpreter the relationship of space, time, ceremony, and stories, Bears Arm (MHA Nation) offers an analogy of the relationship between ceremony and space-time: '[Bears Arm] compares the ceremonies to knots on a string; all are independent ceremonies just as each knot is independent of the other knots, but, at the same time, they are connected and related in the same way that knots are related to each other by their order on the string.'" The Bears Arm quotation appears in Alfred W. Bowers, *Mandan Social and Ceremonial Organization* (University of Nebraska Press, 1992), 30.

19   Furlan, "Wendy Red Star's Archival Interventions."

20   For more on these artists' archival interventions, see Hulleah J. Tsinhnahjinnie, "When Is a Photograph Worth a Thousand Words?" in *Photography's Other Histories*, ed. Christopher Pinney and Nicolas Peterson (Duke University Press, 2003), 40-52, a critical essay by a Seminole-Muscogee-Navajo photographer examining Indigenous photographic practices and representation; Emily C. Burns, "In our Hands: Native Photography, 1890 to Now, October 22, 2023 - January 14, 2024, Minneapolis Institute of Art," *Transatlantica* 1 (2023), which analyzes Catherine Blackburn's technique of beading onto photographic images in her work "But There's No Scar?" (2017); and Deborah A. Miranda, *Bad Indians: A Tribal Memoir* (Heyday, 2013), a mixed-genre memoir incorporating archival photographs, poetry, and personal narrative to reclaim Indigenous history.

21   Jolene Rickard's influential work on "visual sovereignty" has been critical in theorizing Indigenous Peoples' assertion of self-determination through visual media and representation. See Rickard, "Sovereignty: A Line in the Sand," 51-54.

22   Professor Charles Francis Himes offered his services to the Indian School through lectures and conducted several in 1880. Himes used his lectures under the belief that "there are still bigger things to be found further on, and the White Man is still going on," wanting to "explain to them the secret of the White Man's superiority." "An Account of Illustrated Talks to Noted Indian Chiefs," by Charles Francis Himes, https://carlisleindian.dickinson.edu/publications/account-illustrated-talks-noted-indian-chiefs-charles-francis-himes.

23   James Andrew McCauley, while serving as President of Dickinson College (1872-1888), was simultaneously a member of the Executive Committee of the Board of Trustees of the Carlisle Indian School Charity Fund. Archival records document that this Board was "authorized to act in all matters pertaining to the Trust" and show multiple contracts between McCauley, Robert M. Henderson, and Richard Henry Pratt for the lease of the Hocker Farm to the Carlisle Indian School between 1883-1889. See "School Farms - Land Transactions" and "Charity Fund - Board of Trustees," Carlisle Indian School Digital Resource Center, https://carlisleindian.dickinson.edu/topics/school-farms-land-transactions and https://carlisleindian.dickinson.edu/topics/charity-fund-board-trustees.

24   The collaborative relationship between Dickinson College and the Carlisle Indian Industrial School lasted almost four decades, from CIIS's opening in 1879 until its closure in 1918. During this period, "Dickinson College professors served as chaplains and special faculty to the Native American students" and "Dickinson College students volunteered services, observed teaching methods, and participated in events at the Indian School." This institutional collaboration was ongoing in 1901 when the Kritz property was acquired. See 'Reclaiming History,' Dickinson College, July 22, 2014, https://www.dickinson.edu/news/article/1145/reclaiming_history. Cumberland County Recorder of Deeds, "Deed of Sale from Dickinson College to Keystone Arms Associates, LLC," September 17, 2004, Cumberland County Deed Book 265, 2860-2862, Instrument #200440222

25   https://carlisleindianschool.org/, the early website began by Landis and collaborator Genevieve Bell in 1993, wherein Landis notes "Our express purpose in keeping this history alive is to encourage historians to invigorate a troubling conversation and to deliver the Carlisle Indian School student names to their respective nations." Jim Gerencser notes, "Barb's extensive work, still available online after 30 years, highlights her decades of effort before the CISDRC even launched."

26   On archives as sites of power and potential transformation, see Ann Laura Stoler, "Colonial Archives and the Arts of Governance," *Archival Science* 2, no. 1-2 (2002): 87-109, which reconceptualizes colonial archives as "sites of knowledge production" rather than neutral repositories. Jacques Derrida, *Archive Fever: A Freudian Impression*, trans. Eric Prenowitz (University of Chicago Press, 1996), 4-12, provides foundational theory on archives as spaces of power that simultaneously preserve and produce authority. For Indigenous approaches to archival transformation, see Michelle Caswell, "Teaching to Dismantle White Supremacy in Archives," *The Library Quarterly* 87, no. 3 (July 2017): 222-235, which examines how critical engagement with archives can disrupt colonial power structures.

WENDY RED STAR'S ARCHIVAL INTERVENTIONS

LAURA M. FURLAN

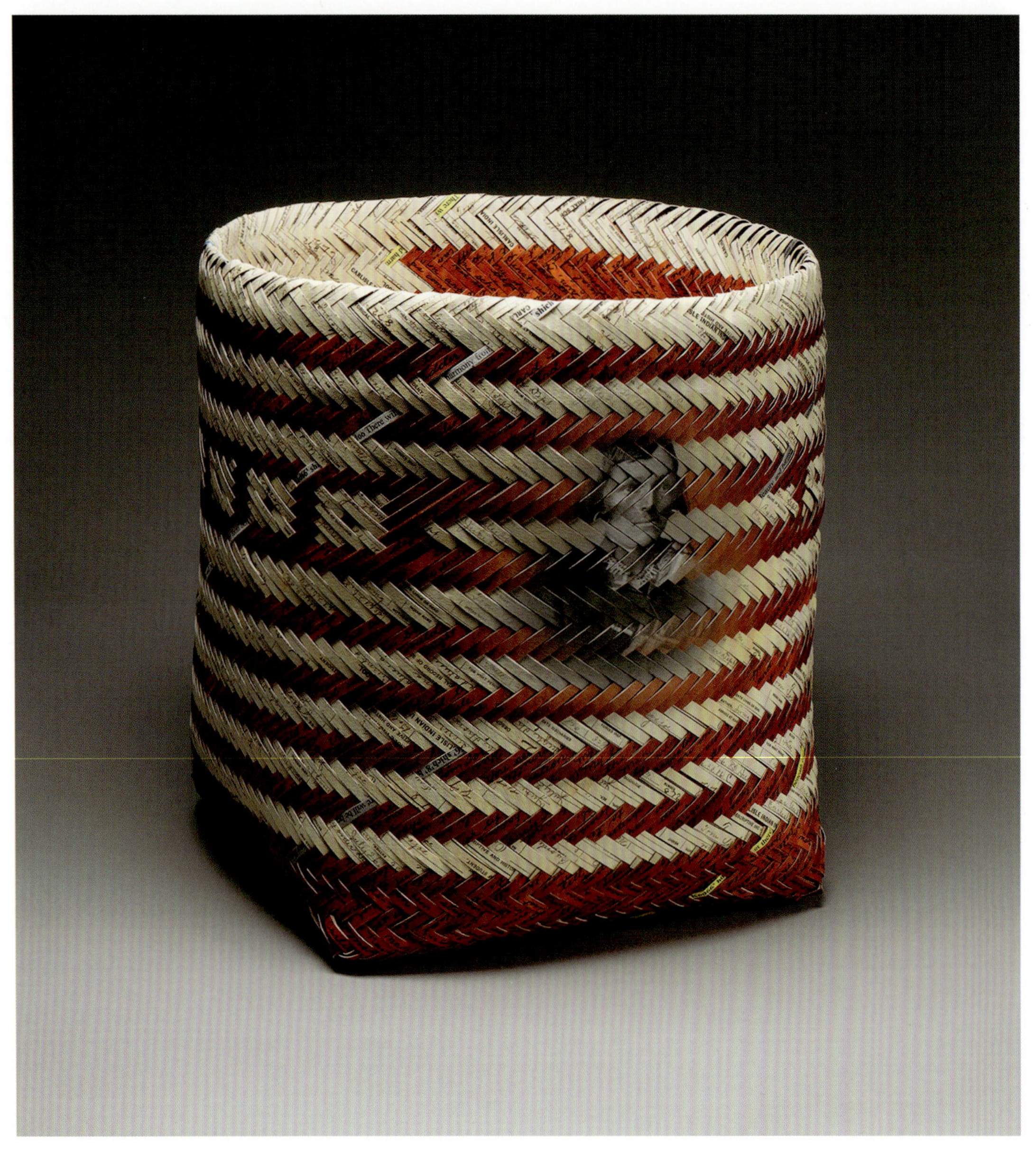

(fig. 1) Shan Goshorn (Eastern Band Cherokee, 1957 – 2018), *Two Views*

2018

Basket from Arches watercolor paper, archival inks, acrylic paint, artificial sinew

14.25 x 13.5 x 13.5 in. (36.2 x 34.29 x 34.29 cm)

Purchase of the Friends of The Trout Gallery, 2018.2

© Estate of Shan Goshorn

WENDY RED STAR'S ARCHIVAL INTERVENTIONS

LAURA M. FURLAN

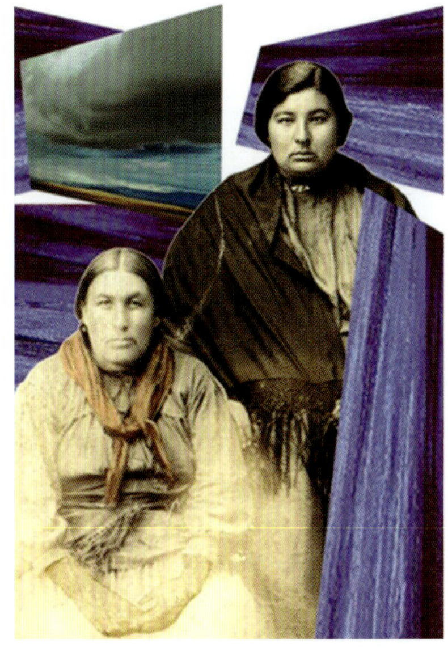

(fig. 2) Hulleah J. Tsinhnahjinnie
(Seminole/Muskogee/Diné, b. 1954),
Oklahoma

2003

© Hulleah J. Tsinhnahjinnie

Multimedia Apsáalooke artist Wendy Red Star "defi[es] convention in everything she does," writes journalist Chuck Thompson.[1] Red Star's work often critiques representations of Native peoples in popular culture and American art, as an "interruption" and "refusal" of the anthropological gaze, to invoke anthropologist Audra Simpson.[2] She sometimes uses an autobiographical self, as in, the one behind and in front of the camera, the one with the proverbial red pen in the *Delegation* series, and the one holding Crow heritage objects in the *Bíiluuke* prints. Her aesthetic is often wildly colorful, using what she calls the "Crow palette," and it relies upon assemblage and collage.[3] Red Star understands the power of the visual and of "visual sovereignty," art historian Jolene Rickard's term for work that promotes the agency of representations of Indigenous people.[4] In her guest-edited issue of *Aperture*, Red Star writes, "I became aware that photography was more than a tool to document—it could also tell powerful stories."[5] The stories she tells in her photographs and in other media illuminate life on the Crow Reservation in Montana and celebrate Apsáalooke history and culture, primarily through acts of preservation and engagement with archives.

Art historians and archivists date the archival turn in art to the 1990s, practiced especially by artists from communities that did not see themselves accurately portrayed in the colonial institutional record.[6] Archival art became a way to engage with memory practices, historiography, and knowledge production. For Indigenous artists, the archival turn follows years of Indigenous archival advocacy, powerfully articulated by Vine Deloria, Jr. in the late 1970s.[7] This archival movement, writes historian Jennifer O'Neal, fought both for access to and then return of documents and cultural belongings held in institutional collections.[8] Indigenous archival art often engages with historical photographs, like Eastern Band Cherokee artist Shan Goshorn's *Resisting the Mission, Filling the Silence* baskets (displayed in an exhibition at The Trout Gallery in 2018). In *Two Views*, Goshorn weaves together reproductions of John Choate's famous nineteenth-century "before and after" photographs of Carlisle Indian Industrial School student Tom Torlino with his biography handwritten by his descendent and reproductions of his CIIS student records (fig. 1).[9] Diné photographer Hulleah Tsinhnahjinnie's *Portraits Against Amnesia* (2003) (fig. 2) also exemplifies this powerful archival turn. In her work, Tsinhnahjinnie recuperates and pairs obscure historical photographs from turn-of-the-century postcards with family photographs in collages, in a move that "constructs intimacy and restores narrative importance to otherwise anonymous images," writes art historian Emma Doubt.[10] While these two artists turn historical photographs into art, Indigenous photographers like Patrice Hall-Walters (Umatilla)—and, as we will see, Wendy Red Star—also turn their cameras to heritage objects in museums, not simply as documentation but to incorporate historical records as part of their artistic practice. Beginning in the late 1990s, Hall-Walters photographed historical beadwork and then baskets, focusing on the minute details of each piece. The works of these archival artists gather sometimes-fraught histories and signify on those histories, bringing pointed attention to the history of archival collections.[11]

Red Star literally takes the archive into her own hands—the historical photographs, wax recordings, allotment maps, ledger art, and heritage objects that she annotates, repurposes, remediates, meticulously cuts out, or photographs in her hand. Archival access is critical to her work—the collections that she's explored at the National Museum of the American Indian (NMAI), the National Anthropological Archives (NAA), and the National Museum of Natural History (NMNH).[12] Red Star's engagement with the archive seems to have started in earnest in 2018 with a Smithsonian Artist's Research Fellowship, though she has always been obsessed with images and photographs and Crow material culture.[13] She explains in an interview with *Truth in Photography:* "The work that I'm doing has a lot of purpose beyond just my own personal interests. It really is for the future generations. I'm really hoping that they can use my work as a starting place, that they don't have to work as hard to gather things together, because I'm trying to do that for them."[14] Incorporating these archival finds into her work makes them accessible to a wider audience, and at the same time it draws attention to the collections themselves—what has been preserved, by whom, and why—and it makes a powerful statement about the value of archives, Indigenous praxis, and ethnographic refusal.

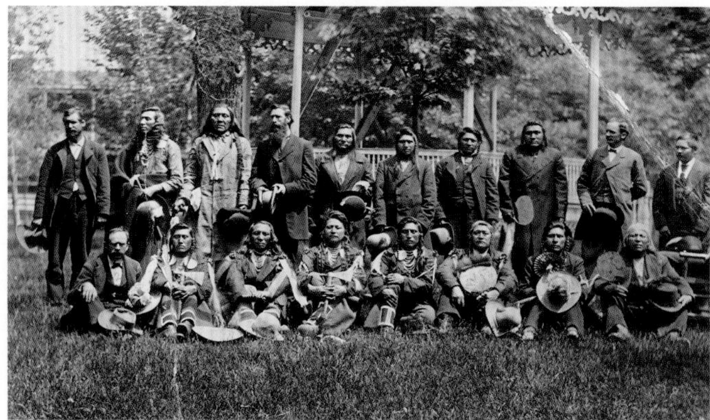

(**fig. 3**) Photographer unknown, Group Portrait of Apsáalooke and Bannock Delegations at the Carlisle Indian School

1880

Photograph

5 x 8.5 in. (12.7 x 21.6 cm)

Denver Public Library, Western History and Genealogy Department, X-31215.

1880 Crow Peace Delegation

Red Star's *1880 Crow Peace Delegation* series consists of ten digitally manipulated archival photographs that have been annotated extensively by Red Star with what appears to be red pen or Sharpie.[15] These photographs of five delegates (front and side views) were made during a treaty delegation to Washington, DC to negotiate land cessions with President Hayes by Charles Milton Bell, a well-known portrait photographer, for the Bureau of Ethnology [then, as part of the U.S. Geological Survey of the Territories].[16] The staged images were taken in a studio and conform to conventions of nineteenth-century photographic portraiture, though they were meant to document the visit rather than to share with relatives and friends, in contrast to most middle-class portraits of that time period. As ethnographic photographs, they were intended to capture the "exotic" nature of these men and not necessarily their individual personalities; however, Red Star's annotations demonstrate how the leaders' choices of clothing and adornment reveal much about them.

Inviting tribal delegates to the nation's capital was intended as both a gesture of friendship and a show of force—demonstrating the nation's military power to discourage resistance.[17] Indigenous leaders and representatives were frequently invited by local reservation agents to visit the capital, where they were given tours of the city and often received presidential medals and gifts of clothing. Delegations came to Washington to negotiate peace treaties, land disputes and forfeitures, and rights of way for the railroad (which was the purpose of this trip). Arriving with the intention to represent the rights of their people, tribal leaders pleaded their cases to the president and other government officials. They often traveled a long way, during the winter months, when Congress was in session. The Apsáalooke delegation in 1880 was in the capital for nearly two months; they traveled first by wagon and then by train, stopping over in Chicago. On their way home, on May 18, 1880, the delegation visited Carlisle Indian Industrial School and posed for a group photograph (fig. 3).[18] The first group of Apsáalooke students arrived at the school in February 1883, and Alexander Upshaw,

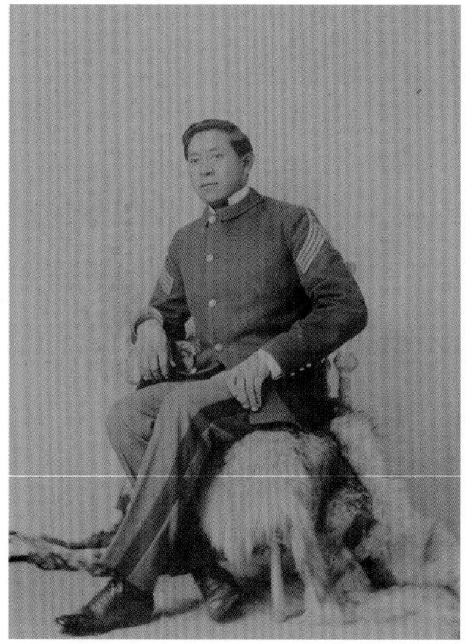

(**fig. 4**) John N. Choate, *Alexander Upshaw*

c. 1891

Photograph

3.86 x 5.44 in. (9.8 x 13.8 cm)

Cumberland County Historical Society, Carlisle, Pennsylvania

Laura M. Furlan

who would go on to work as a translator for Edward S. Curtis on his *The North American Indian* project, came to Carlisle in 1888 (fig 4).[19]

In her study of Native photography, art historian Nicole Strathman describes historical Native photographs such as these delegation ones as "destined for the archives." She also calls attention to not just the intent of their taking and their collection (and perhaps their later distribution and circulation), but also to the images as archival objects, which Red Star's manipulation does not mask.[20] Some of the images, for example the side view of Medicine Crow, are damaged by their age (fig 5). A few of the prints suggest the original glass plate negatives may have cracked; tape marks appear as lighter squares atop the photograph. These flaws are seen in the Medicine Crow side-view, along with a large crack that runs from the lower left side that curves all the way to the top. While Red Star may not emphasize the cracks or repairs or gradations in color, she does not remove them through her digital manipulations of the photographs (although she crops the top of the photo just a little). In other words, the images' imperfections are critical to their composition, and they are reminders of the photograph as archive, and that we are encountering them as such. Red Star's work asserts that these are indeed historical images that have been preserved, catalogued, and damaged along the way.

Red Star's intervention and use of red ink—which can be read as a corrective— immediately draws the eye to the text, then slowly to the photographic image. Her annotations, which include the outlining of certain items of dress and fashion, highlight the absence of Apsáalooke context and knowledge by the photographer and carefully consider the articles of clothing that each person is wearing, their relationships, social positions, and life dates to reclaim their humanity from the historical and ethnographic lens. Red Star traces items like hair bows ("out of fashion by 1880," she writes), eagle feathers (some held, some in hair, signifying bravery in battle), shell earrings, strips of ermine attached to sleeves and pant legs, hair extensions, weapons, and moccasin designs. Red Star explains that the outlining began as a way for her to see details more closely, to bring those details into sharper focus, and to represent the results of her research.[21] With her red ink, she is teaching us how to read those archival photographs, not through their original colonial framing, but through an Apsáalooke lens.

Red Star's insertion and assertion of text in red ink onto a historical photograph *changes* the image. The act of writing words onto the photograph is simultaneously an act of resistance, of revision, of conversation, and of care. The resistance, as I have already suggested, is a thwarting of the ethnographic gaze, in defiance to the silence of the original image, an opposition to the surveillance of the state. The outlining of details adds a dimension to the flattened image, and the color red gives life to these black-and-white photos, bringing these five men out of the past and into the present. I also read this red as a conversation with the image, demonstrated most clearly with the speech bubbles she gives to four of the five men. A speech bubble on Plenty Coups's front view photograph (fig. 6), for example, reads "Alaxchiiaahush," as though he is speaking his own name. Red Star has drawn a line from the bubble to Plenty Coup's mouth, a convention found in ledger art, a practice most commonly associated with Plains Indigenous peoples who used ledger and accounting paper to record stories and scenes of everyday life during a period of forced assimilation.

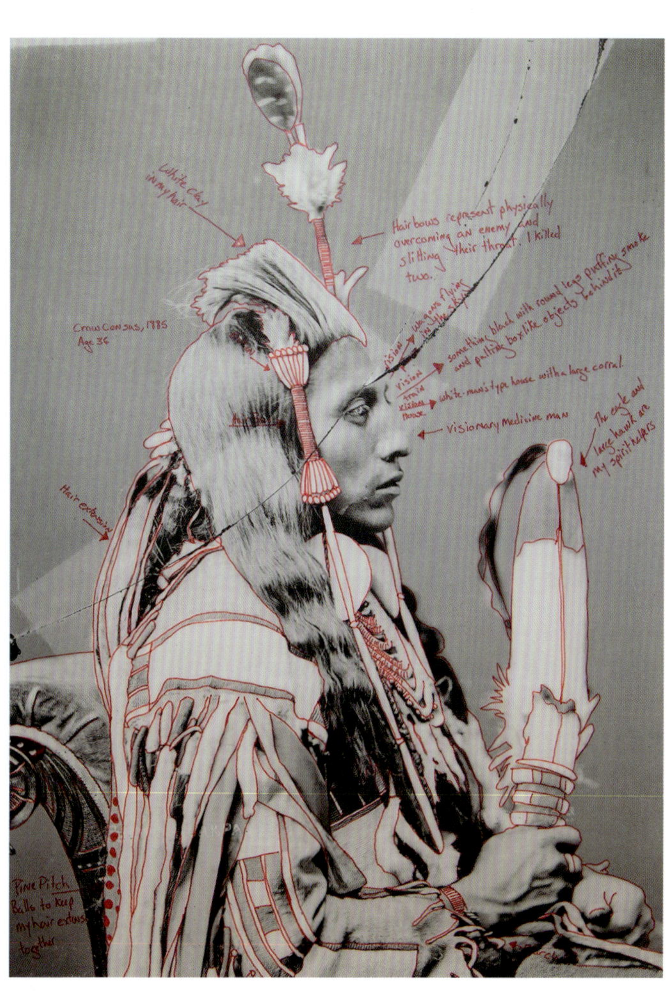

(fig. 5) Wendy Red Star
(Apsáalooke (Crow), born 1981),
*Peelatchiwaaxpáash / Medicine Crow
(Raven)*

2014

Artist-manipulated digitally reproduced photograph by C.M. (Charles Milton) Bell, National Anthropological Archives, Smithsonian Institution

25 × 17 in. (63.5 × 43.2 cm)

Image courtesy of the artist and Sargent's Daughters © Wendy Red Star

This speech act serves as a declaration of personhood and of kinship, as naming oneself is always connected to naming one's family. Red Star gives these men the power to speak their names in Apsáalooke, replacing the English translations that officially name the historical photographs in the archive. Her red ink is a connection to Crow aesthetics, both with the nod to ledger art and in the way that she outlines the Crow designs on their clothing and accessories.

In addition to giving the delegates the agency to speak their *names*, Red Star renames the original photographs as an act of data correction. Bell's side view photograph of Medicine Crow, for example, is titled *Perits-Shinakpas or Paretche-Mark-Bosh, Called Medicine Crow*, and the seated photograph of Medicine Crow is called *Crow Man, Medicine Crow in Native Dress with Ornaments and Holding Fan* in the National Anthropological Archives. Red Star's image pair is retitled *Peelatchiwaaxpáash/Medicine Crow (Raven)*, which, like her red ink, also serves as an historical corrective, by both using the accurate Apsáalooke name for him and a more accurate translation (*Raven*, not *Crow*). Her intervention here is subtle, and a viewer might not even notice it without consulting the original images, but naming is important work, as is the language work involved in correcting a badly transliterated name into Apsáalooke. The gesture conveys care and respect for these ancestors and performs a political act that delves into debates about Native names and languages.[22]

Red Star's red ink also calls attention to the choices the delegates made regarding clothing and accessories. Strathmore writes about the participation of Native sitters as "agents in their own representations," that we need to take into account their "motivation and desires for self-representation."[23] We can imagine that the delegates wore the finest clothing that they had brought along on that long trip. Two Belly wears a jacket with buttons that was popular with the River Crow, according to Red Star's annotations (fig. 7). Plenty Coup holds an axe and wears a conch shell earring. Medicine Crow holds an eagle feather and wears moccasins with a "buffalo impound design." Old Crow wears a "military inspired coat" and a Nez Perce necklace (fig. 8). Red Star notes that he participated in Buffalo Bill's Wild West Show four years after this photograph was taken. His arm is outstretched to highlight the many attached strands of ermine on his sleeves. His hand rests on something just outside the frame, a cane or another chair. Pretty Eagle also holds an axe as a prop (it could be the same one) and wears large conch shell earrings (fig. 9). They may have felt important to be sitting for these photographs. Perhaps they struggled to keep a deadpan expression while their fellow delegates sit outside the frame, making jokes about how important they look, or they were hungry, or frustrated with the negotiations, or missing home. The studio could have been too warm or too cold, and they could have regretted their choices of clothing. The photographs may have captured them on glass plate negatives, but the delegation made many of their own choices in front of the camera. They, too, wanted to be remembered for their negotiations with the U.S. government and meeting with the president, for being Apsáalooke representatives and tribal leaders.

(fig. 6) Wendy Red Star (Apsáalooke (Crow), born 1981), *Alaxchiiaahush / Many War Achievements / Plenty Coups*

2014

Artist-manipulated digitally reproduced photograph by C.M. (Charles Milton) Bell, National Anthropological Archives, Smithsonian Institution

25 × 17 in. (63.5 × 43.2 cm)

Image courtesy of the artist and Sargent's Daughters © Wendy Red Star

(fig. 7) Wendy Red Star (Apsáalooke (Crow), born 1981), *Bia Eélisaash/Large Stomach Woman (Pregnant Woman) / Two Belly*

2014

Artist-manipulated digitally reproduced photograph by C.M. (Charles Milton) Bell, National Anthropological Archives, Smithsonian Institution

25 × 17 in. (63.5 × 43.2 cm)

Image courtesy of the artist and Sargent's Daughters © Wendy Red Star

(fig. 8) Wendy Red Star (Apsáalooke (Crow), born 1981), *Peelatchixaaliash / Old Crow (Raven)*

2014

Artist-manipulated digitally reproduced photograph by C.M. (Charles Milton) Bell, National Anthropological Archives, Smithsonian Institution

25 × 17 in. (63.5 × 43.2 cm)

Image courtesy of the artist and Sargent's Daughters © Wendy Red Star

(fig. 9) Wendy Red Star (Apsáalooke (Crow), born 1981), *Déaxitchish / Pretty Eagle*

2014

Artist-manipulated digitally reproduced photograph by C.M. (Charles Milton) Bell, National Anthropological Archives, Smithsonian Institution

25 × 17 in. (63.5 × 43.2 cm).

Image courtesy of the artist and Sargent's Daughters © Wendy Red Star

Red Star's use of the information usually found on a museum wall label, the catalog number in the title, and the "Description" and "Tribe" lines, further her reckoning with the ethnographic practices at work in the museum space. The description in the Denver Art Museum catalog identifies this item as "Cradle"; Red Star inserts the Apsáalooke word into her description, updating it as a corrective (but without the red ink of *Delegation*). This intervention is consistent throughout the series; each object is renamed, and in this way Red Star enters into a dialogue with the taxonomy that is represented by the card. The inclusion of "Tribe: Crow" is a reminder of ethnographic and museum categories; although the Denver Art Museum names the artist in this instance, institutional information about Indigenous makers is often absent. In art writer Taylor Defoe's words about another series, *Travels Pretty*, which reimagines the designs on parfleches that Red Star also found in museums, Red Star "often makes liberal use of labels, captions, and annotations, appropriating the kind of taxonomical language so often used to portray her culture."[29]

In Red Star's *Catalogue Number 1938.52*, the orientation of the cradleboard is vertical on the yellow index card (though the single hole at the bottom of the card indicates it would sit horizontally in a drawer). Fringe hangs from the top and the bottom of the cradleboard. An unbeaded portion indicates where a baby's head would rest; otherwise, stripes, diamonds, triangles of red, blue, green, yellow, and pink comprise the cradleboard's design.[30] The contemporary photograph seen at the bottom of Red Star's composition is of a woman on a horse at Crow Fair. The colors of her regalia, particularly her pink elk tooth dress, the green and red of her saddle blanket, and the lined and triangular patterns, resonate with the vibrant cradle. This likeness affirms the continuity of Indigenous artistic practices, between the style of the nineteenth-century cradle artwork and the contemporary Crow Fair regalia. The visual story that Red Star tells in this digital collage is about the endurance of Apsáalooke material culture and designs.[31]

At the same time, the prints in this series highlight and celebrate contemporary powwow culture—the traditions and regalia still in use today. Another definition of "accession" is about joining, which makes me think about the connection between the representations of these objects in the museum and current Apsáalooke patterns and designs. This joining or collaging serves as a merging of past and present, a collapsing of time, while also celebrating a vibrant, living culture and serving as a kind of visual repatriation or rematriation of the material culture items.[32] Red Star emphasizes the visual repetition between the prints, of the patterns, colors, and designs of the historical items and the clothing worn at Crow Fair. Red Star imaginatively takes the historical items *out* of the museum and into the contemporary reservation space, where they can be cared for and worn and celebrated. Red Star's work brings these items home, to Crow Fair. Of course, this resonates with the kinds of reckoning happening among museums with Indigenous belongings in their collections in the wake of recent revisions to improve the implementation of NAGPRA (Native American Graves Protection and Repatriation Act).[33]

Red Star's *Accession* series also draws attention to the outdated technology of the card catalog, the taxonomy of order, and the "descriptive apparatus" that together define collecting culture.[34] Like the tape marks on the *Medicine Crow* negative, Red Star preserves the imperfections of the catalog card—the creases in the corners, the fingerprints and

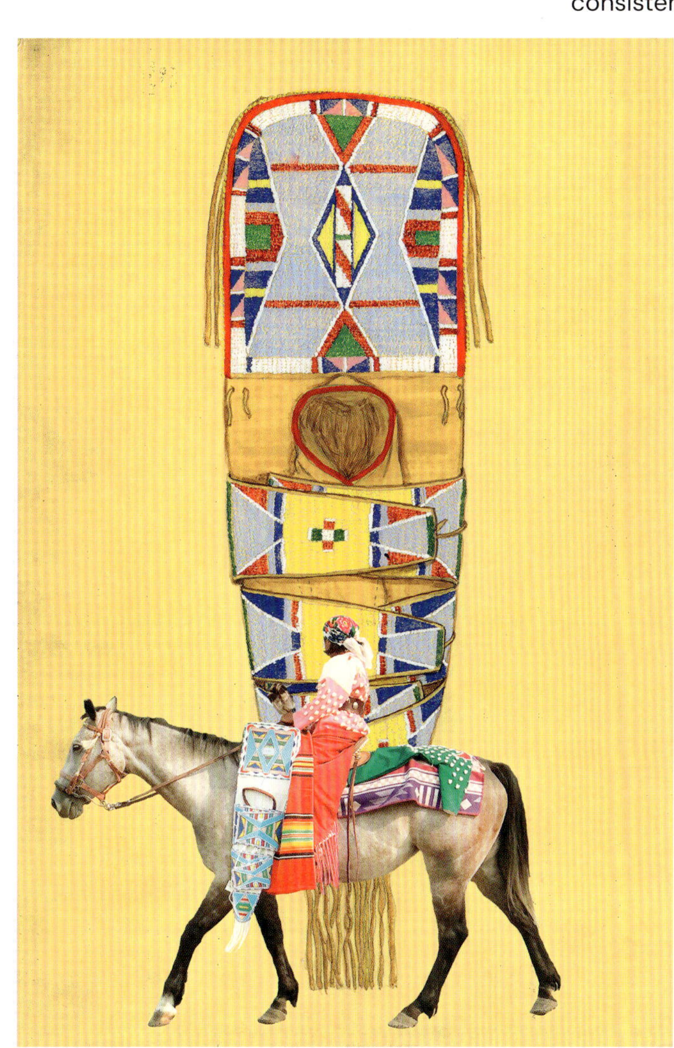

(**fig. 11**) Wendy Red Star (Apsáalooke (Crow), born 1981), *Catalogue Number 1938.52*

2019

Pigment print on archival paper, edition 1 of 10 and 2 AP

28 x 18 in. (71.1 x 45.7 cm)

Image courtesy of the artist and Sargent's Daughters © Wendy Red Star

smudges (particularly at what would be the top of the card) that show its age and use. The only feature that she does edit out in this one in particular is the hole on the bottom of the card, where it would be held in place by a metal rod in a drawer, to keep the cards in order. Removing the hole feels symbolic, as if untethering the card from the drawer in which it has been held.[35]

These cards are extraordinary: a pre-internet card catalog typically contained 4 x 6 index cards, holes at the bottom, with text pointing to an object's location and perhaps additional information about the object, but they rarely have handmade graphic renditions of the collection.[36] The images are strikingly beautiful, meticulously drawn, and painted with care. Red Star admits she was jealous that the anonymous illustrators employed through the Museum Extensions Project spent so much time with these belongings—maybe even that they were touched by their hands. These cards are like an intermediary between the collection and the artist—one step removed from the cultural heritage belongings at the museum—but still very much representative of them. They speak to a kind of close proximity that museum staff and these mid-twentieth-century artists had with the heritage objects, access that regular museum visitors and Apsáalooke community members may not have had.[37]

Bíiluuke (Our Side)

Bíiluuke (Our Side) is a series of photographs of Apsáalooke heritage objects (most of them accessioned at NMAI) in Red Star's hands, against a white background.[38] The trappings of the museum are visible in some of the images—identifying tags, like the card catalogs discussed above, which are markers of collecting and ownership. The items are being touched—allowed for tribal members at NMAI (as an unofficial policy) but unheard of at many modern institutions.[39] While early museums often functioned as cabinets of curiosities that encouraged privileged visitors and collectors to touch the objects in the collection, a shift to preservation protocol in the modern era discourages object handling. The images of Apsáalooke objects in Red Star's hand call for experiencing the items in this tactile way; the works are a reminder that one cannot feel the items' textures or estimate their heft through sight alone.[40] Holding these objects suggests another way of knowing them, of reaching across the boundaries of archive and time, to be in relationship with them.[41]

A performance piece entitled *We Wear One Another* (2019) by Alutiiq artist Tanya Linklater similarly responds to an Indigenous object held in a major museum collection. Linklater explains, "Our knowledges were felt and held in the body. Our knowledges were activated physically, sonically, in relation to these belongings, to our families, to the land, to the universe."[42] Linklater suggests a method of care and visiting that functions well beyond the visual, that articulates an Indigenous archival practice of visiting with these cultural belongings, of experiencing them with the body.[43] The *Bíiluuke* series also suggests a mode of Indigenous care and handling over the museum's focus on and privileging of preservation.[44]

Some of Red Star's prints depict one object and one hand, like *Issbiiaxcbe (hair tie)*, which features a blue and white beaded circle, hide strings to attach the tie to hair, and four strands of red with white and purple stripes near the bottom.[45] Red Star's hand is palm up, and she holds the top of the item between her thumb and first finger. She wears a silver ring on her

Laura M. Furlan

middle finger, and white nail polish can be seen on her thumb. In *Baatitchi (good things)*, there are two left hands, each holding different objects: on the left, a beaded pink hand, with a white tag dangling; on the right, a beaded item made of strands of hide, white, blue, red, sky blue, and pink beads, with four tufts of white fur at the bottom.[46] In the left image, Red Star wears a brass-colored ring on her ring finger, and her sleeve—red with tiny white polka dots—is barely showing. The hand at the right shows a silver banded bracelet at the wrist. A third image, *Baaihchiiláxiio (jewelry)*, is a grouping or three hands, two left and one right, that are holding a necklace and two bracelets, each made of hide, elk teeth, painted trade beads, and, in the bracelet on the right, long, dark, curved bear claws.[47]

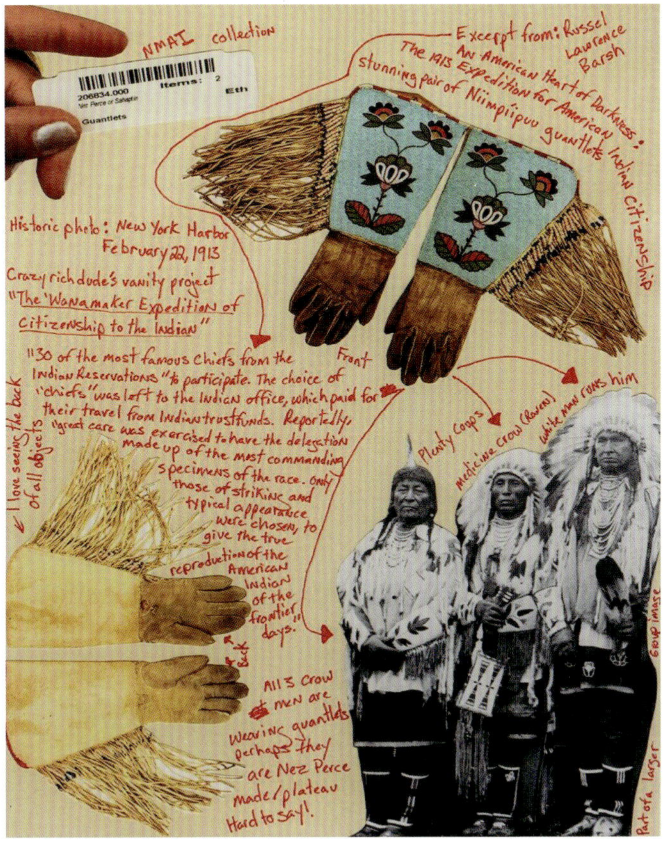

In NMAI's catalog image of the amulet in *Baatitichi (good things)*, one of the fingers is folded under, and a tag attached reads "24/2457 CROW." While there is an inch marker in the corner of the image to indicate its size, it is not entirely clear how small it is until it is pictured in Red Star's hand. In Red Star's photograph, the beaded hand is outstretched, and the tag that hangs below is turned so that the writing is not visible. The turning of the tag feels purposeful, an erasure of the handwritten specimen or accession number in favor of a blank tag—not removed entirely, for the history it represents, but turned away from the camera's eye to keep the focus on the pink hand with its blue horseshoe symbol at its center. According to the accession records, this piece was sold to the Museum of the American Indian (MAI) director Frederick J. Dockstader by a Mrs. Roberts (perhaps of Roberts Indian Crafts and Supplies) in Anandarko, Oklahoma, in 1968. There are no notes about who first purchased or acquired the "charm," how much it cost, whether it could have been stolen, who made it and when, or where it originated. This absence of origin makes this reunion of beaded hand in human hand in Red Star's print even more powerful. The hand, of course, allows for touch and for experiencing the item haptically. It also a meaningful reminder that these items were made by Apsáalooke hands, not just held by them.

Apsáalooke Objects in Collections

Red Star's more recent collages are comprised of historical and contemporary photographs of Apsáalooke people and material culture, some with accession tags attached to them, accompanied by handwritten notes and occasionally with images of Red Star's hand, on different colored backgrounds. These assemblages call to mind that act of bringing things together that Choctaw writer LeAnne Howe describes in her theory of tribalography, the Indigenous compulsion to gather past, present, and future.[48] These collages not only unite the various items pictured, along with Red Star's textual interventions, but they also build on the three series discussed above: *Delegation*, *Accession*, and *Bíiluuke (Our Side)*.

In the upper left corner of *huxshé (glove)* (fig. 12), Red Star's fingers can be seen holding a white tag with a bar code that below reads:

> 206834.000   Items: 2
> *Nez Perce or Sahaptin*   Eth
> Gauntlets[49]

(fig. 12) Wendy Red Star (Apsáalooke (Crow), born 1981), *Set A: huxshé (glove)*

2023

Archival pigment print on Satin Photo Rag, edition 1 of 3

20.5 x 16 in.

Image courtesy of the artist and Sargent's Daughters © Wendy Red Star

Written above the tag in Red Star's red marker is "NMAI collection." To the right is a cut-out photograph of the gauntlets, made of hide, beaded extensively on the wrist portions, a flower pattern on a sky-blue background, and fringe off the sides. A black-and-white photograph of three Crow men—Plenty Coup, Medicine Crow (Raven), and White Man Runs Him—in the lower-right corner also includes a handwritten comment indicating this is part of a larger group photograph. On the left, a photograph of the back of the gauntlets appears with Red Star's note: "I love seeing the back of all objects." In the spaces between the images, Red Star has written extensively in red ink.[50] She records the date and place of the historic photograph: New York Harbor, February 22, 1913 and includes an excerpt from a book about this particular delegation, "The Wanamaker Expedition of Citizenship to the Indian." At the bottom she writes, "All 3 Crow men are wearing guantlets (sic). Perhaps they are Nez Perce made/Plateau Hard to say!"

As in Red Star's other series, this collage insists on access and context. Red Star studied these gloves at NMAI and photographed them herself; the image in the online NMAI catalog shows the gauntlets reversed, so that the fringe overlaps in the middle (and, of course, there is no photograph of the backs of the gloves).[51] And while the gauntlets are presumed to be Niimpíipuu (Nez Perce), the men in the photograph appear to be wearing very similar ones, perhaps received as gifts or through trade, pointing to the need for access to collections and metadata beyond those attributed to a tribe or region. This composition also works as a reckoning of ethnographic processes of the museum, the tracking and commodification indicated by bar codes. The story that Red Star illustrates here reminds us that historical context is everything, that collecting and collections are complicated.

The items pictured in these collages are not just housed at NMAI; Red Star finds Apsáalooke belongings at the Denver Art Museum, the Montana Historical Society, the National Museum of Natural History, the University of Montana, Newark Museum of Art, Denver Public Library, and the National Anthropological Archives. Red Star is careful to name these locations and the sources of her images. For instance, in *buffalo = bishée* and *coat = baleiítaashteeiwische* one of the images of Curley in a buffalo coat on a horse is noted "Photo source unknown (fucking pinterest)," and another note reads, "Actually I found the photo source! Forsyth, N.A. (Norman A), 1869-1949 MHS," in a different colored ink. Red Star crossed out her original notes in two places in this collage and provides updated information; first, she corrects "Curly" to "Curley" and "Buffalo coat" to "Bearskin???." What I find interesting about these textual edits is how she documents the process of gathering, the messy act of assemblage. She also draws arrows to connect the items, in this collage and others, providing visual linkages between words and pictures.

In *isshulúuwate (tin armband)* (fig. 13), two beaded armbands on hide from the collection of the Denver Art Museum, dated 1930, are arranged in a parallel angle across the top of the image. Below the armbands are the following items: a note on the back of a photograph of Boy in the Water from the National Anthropological Archives, a photograph of Spotted Horse and Snake from the Montana Historical Society, the titular tin armband from the NMAI collection photographed in Red Star's hand, and a second photograph of Spotted Horse from the Denver Public Library collection. The men in the historical photographs all wear tin armbands, which are noted by Red Star's hand-drawn arrows. In handwritten text next to the image of the NMAI armband, Red Star tells the story of how Native people used metal

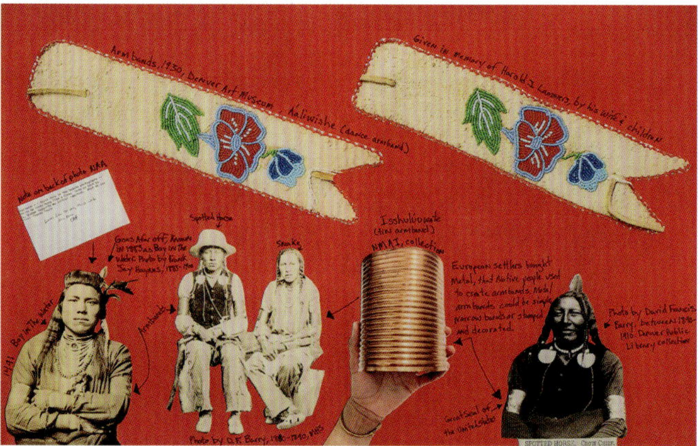

(fig. 13) Wendy Red Star (Apsáalooke (Crow), born 1981), S*et E: isshulúuwate (tin armband)*

2023

Archival pigment print on Satin Photo Rag, edition 1 of 3

16 x 25 in (40.64 x 63.5 cm)

Image courtesy of the artist and Sargent's Daughters © Wendy Red Star

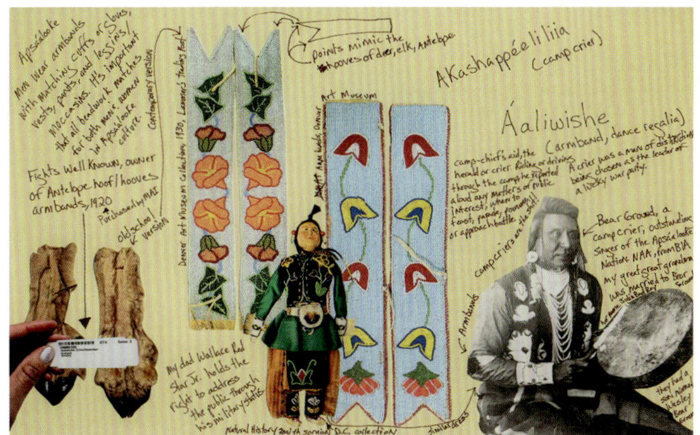

(fig. 14) Wendy Red Star
(Apsáalooke (Crow), born 1981), *Set E:
akashappéeliliia (camp crier)*

2023

Archival pigment print on Satin Photo
Rag, edition 1 of 3

16 x 25 in. (40.64 x 63.5 cm)

Image courtesy of the artist and
Sargent's Daughters © Wendy Red Star

from settlers to make these decorative pieces. The collage is both a curating *of* archives and *about* archiving: the note on the back of the NAA photograph of Boy in the Water reveals that the image had been filed with Dakota materials, though "he looks more like a Crow," writes one archivist. Red Star's gathering reveals and corrects this misfiling, as she visually points to the armband as evidence of his Crow-ness.

Red Star arranges other examples of armbands—antelope hoof armbands from NMAI and two sets of beaded armbands from the Denver Art Museum—in *akashappéeliliia (camp crier)* (fig. 14). Her notes explain that the two points on one side of the armbands "mimic the hooves of deer, elk, antelope," a recognizable Crow aesthetic. Between the sets of beaded armbands is a doll (pictured in color) from the Natural History Smithsonian DC collection, and to the right is a cut-out of a historical photograph from the NAA of Bear Ground, a camp crier. Bear Ground wears an armband, and Red Star points out that he and the doll are wearing similar clothing. Red Star offers extensive notes about the role of the camp crier, how Bear Ground was married to Red Star's great-great-grandmother Julia Bad Boy, and how Red Star's father "holds the right to address the public through his military status," as an extension of camp criers for contemporary Apsáalooke people.

The collages in this series place cultural belongings alongside historical photographs and documents. Red Star holds many of these objects in her hand, like in the *Bíiluuke* prints, picturing them in Crow hands. She also allows us to see often hidden sides of items, like the gauntlets, or the note on the back of the NAA photograph. Holding and turning them over, Red Star's gestures convey a sense of intimacy, as she puts Apsáalooke belongings and practices into a web of relationships with other belongings and with her relatives. Ultimately, Red Star asserts that the archive is a site of relations. Red Star is *righting* the archive in this series. She not only connects the belongings but also reminds us (and them) where they belong.

The works in these four series—*1880 Crow Peace Delegation*, *Accession*, *Bíiluuke (Our Side)*, and *Apsáalooke Objects in Collections*—are active, performative engagements with archival collections. Red Star explains, "In one way, I am trying to build this counter-archive that is accessible and makes sense of my own living experience. I feel like I am the counter-archive."[52] In her construction of an alternate archive, Red Star gathers documents, photographs, and material culture items from a variety of institutions and demonstrates a new way of organizing from across collections and time periods and geographies. Her artistic practice refuses the ethnographic lens and settler containment, through reanimating historical items in the present. She shows us the difficult work of undoing and un-cata-loguing settler logics and entanglements. Furthermore, she articulates Indigenous care and visiting protocols in archival and museum spaces. As archivist, activist, and artist, she asks us to view these materials through an Apsáalooke lens and to imagine a future when these items might be returned home. And thus, her archival futures involve greater potential for the rematriation of items in these collections, of deaccession and Indigenous stewardship, of expanded access to collections by a greater number of people, and the inclusion of Indigenous knowledges and practices in archival and museum spaces. Red Star's archival work is revolutionary.

NOTES

1 Chuck Thompson, "Wendy Red Star and the Indigenous Voice," *Cowboys and Indians*, January 25, 2018, https://www.cowboysindians.com/2018/01/wendy-red-star-and-the-indigenous-voice/.

2 Audra Simpson, *Mohawk Interruptus* (Duke University Press, 2014), 97. Simpson writes, "Within Indigenous contexts, when the people speak for themselves, their sovereignty interrupts anthropological portraits of timelessness, procedure, and function that dominate representations of their past and, sometimes, their present."

3 Thompson, "Wendy Red Star and the Indigenous Voice."

4 Jolene Rickard, "Sovereignty: A Line in the Sand," in *Strong Hearts: Native American Visions and Voices*, ed. Peggy Roalf (Aperture, 1995), 50–59. Michelle Raheja also uses the term to discuss Indigenous film. See Michelle H. Raheja, *Reservation Reelism: Redfacing, Visual Sovereignty, and Representations of Native Americans in Film* (University of Nebraska Press, 2011).

5 "Editors' Note: Native America," special issue, "Native America," *Aperture* 240 (2020): 21.

6 Hall Foster, "An Archival Impulse," *October* 110 (2004): 3–22; Sara Callahan, *Art + Archive: Understanding the Archival Turn in Contemporary Art* (Manchester University Press, 2022); Ernst Van Alphen, *Staging the Archive: Art and Photography in the Age of New Media* (Reaktion Books, 2014); Annalisa Laganà, "Archives and Contemporary Art: A Matter of Individuality," *Archivo Papers* 5 (2025): 7–24. https://doi.org/10.5281/zenodo.15757101.

7 Vine Deloria, Jr., *The Right to Know: A Paper* (Office of Library and Information Services, U.S. Department of the Interior, 1978), 13–17.

8 Jennifer O'Neal, "Respect, Recognition and Reciprocity: The Protocols for Native American Archival Materials," in *Identity Palimpsests: Archiving Ethnicity in the U.S. and Canada*, ed. Dominique Daniel and Amalia Levi (Litwin Books, 2014), 125–42.

9 Jacqueline Fear-Segal, "Two-Faced Photographs Regenerated in Warp and Weft: Shan Goshorn's Carlisle Baskets," in *Shan Goshorn: Resisting the Mission*, ed. Phillip Earenfight (The Trout Gallery, 2018), 45–53.

10 Emma Doubt, "Portraits Against Amnesia: Archival Recuperation in the Work of Hulleah J. Tsinhnahjinnie," *World Art* 6, no. 1 (2018): 28.

11 Doubt, "Portraits Against Amnesia." Doubt cites Onondaga artist Jeff Thomas, who writes, "My dream is to make the archive an active site of engagement" and "I came to discover that the images were only in a state of sleep." "Signifying" is a nod to Henry Louis Gates, Jr.'s *Signifying Monkey: A Theory of African-American Literary Criticism* (Twayne, 1988). Signifying refers to the way that authors use motifs from other texts but playfully revise them in order to make new meanings.

12 During her Smithsonian Artist's Research Fellowship in 2018, Red Star spent time at NMAI, the National Anthropological Archives, and the National Museum of Natural History. Wendy Red Star, "People of the Earth: Wendy Red Star in Conversation with Emily Moazami," special issue, "Native America," *Aperture* 240 (2020): 23–31.

13 This, too, is from the first of the *Aperture* recorded talks about Red Star's edited special issue in 2020. See "Aperture Conversations: Inside the 'Native America' Issue with Wendy Red Star and Natalie Diaz," September 17, 2020, https://www.youtube.com/watch?v=1jjxRYtSX1g.

14 "Delegation: Conversation with Wendy Red Star," *Truth in Photography*, (2020), https://www.truthinphotography.org/delegation.html.

15 The images are 25 x 17 in. archival pigment prints on photo paper. Pigment prints are often used to mimic the tone of darkroom photographic prints.

16 Bell's firm C.M. Bell Studio on Pennsylvania Avenue took over the delegation photography in 1867. His work was featured in the 1877 Jackson Catalogue, produced by the U.S. Geological Survey of the Territories. Bell is also known for his photographs of prominent people like Frederick Douglas, Helen Keller, Susan B. Anthony, Mrs. Grover Cleveland, and Alexander Graham Bell. See Paula Richardson Fleming and Judith Luskey, *The North American Indians in Early Photographs* (Harper & Row, 1986), 22; Kathleen Collins, *Washingtoniana: Photographs: Collections in the Prints and Photographs Division of the Library of Congress* (Library of Congress, 1989), 14–22; Wendy Red Star and Shannon Vittoria, "Apsáalooke Bacheeítuuk in Washington, DC: A Case Study in Re-Reading Nineteenth-Century Delegation Photography," *Panorama: Journal of the Association of Historians of American Art* 6, no. 2 (2020), https://doi.org/10.24926/24716839.10672. Red Star and Vittoria suggest that the photoshoot at Bell's studio would have been open to the public; also, that the leaders were probably given prints to take home with them. They have been unable to find photographs of the sixth delegate.

17   Herman J. Viola, *Diplomats in Buckskins: A History of Indian Delegations in Washington City* (Rivilo Books, 1981).

18   The event was recorded in the school newspaper, *Eadle Keatah Toh* 1, no. 3 (1880): 3. The newspaper notes that the Crow leaders did not seem "desirous of any improvement in their mode of life," perhaps suggesting that there was some resistance to sending Crow students to Carlisle. My thanks to Jim Gerencser for this reference, who notes that this appears to be the first delegation to visit the school. Carlisle Indian School Digital Resource Center, Archives and Special Collections, Waidner-Spahr Library, Dickinson College, https://carlisleindian.dickinson.edu/sites/default/files/docs-publications/EKT_v01n03_0.pdf).

19   Red Star and Vittoria, "Apsáalooke Bacheeítuuk in Washington, DC." Red Star and Vittoria write that Upshaw's cultural knowledge made its way into Curtis's book and that Red Star reclaims it in her work—she uses Upshaw's written work specifically in her annotations of the delegation photographs. See also Shamoon Zamir, "Native Agency and the Making of 'The North American Indian': Alexander B. Upshaw and Edward S. Curtis," *American Indian Quarterly* 31, no. 4 (2007): 613-53. Documents in the Carlisle Indian School Digital Resource Center indicate Apsáalooke reluctance in sending students to Carlisle, a delay in getting approval from authorities in Washington, DC, the Bureau of Indian Affairs' desire for students to attend school at Crow Agency, but also perhaps a lack of funding for their travel. Carlisle Indian School Digital Resource Center, Archives and Special Collections, Waidner-Spahr Library, Dickinson College, https://carlisleindian.dickinson.edu/documents/crow-agency-inquiry-how-obtain-students and https://carlisleindian.dickinson.edu/documents/need-crow-nation-be-educated. Thanks again to Jim Gerencser for his help finding these documents.

20 Nicole Dawn Strathman, *Through a Native Lens: American Indian Photography* (University of Oklahoma Press, 2020), 9.

21   "Back to the Blanket: Wendy Red Star in Conversation with Josh T. Franco," in *Wendy Red Star: Delegation* (Aperture, 2022), 32.

22   The Indigenous archives movement has prompted efforts among archivists to develop protocols and best practices for Indigenous naming and cataloguing of materials. See Allison Boucher Krebs, "Native America's Twenty-First Century Right to Know," *Archival Science* 12, no. 2, (2012): 173-90; O'Neal, "Respect, Recognition and Reciprocity." One might also think of the controversy over the renaming of places, like Mount McKinley to Denali, a decades-long dispute that ended in legislation signed by Obama in 2015, only to be recently reversed by the Trump administration.

23 Strathman, *Through a Native Lens*, 9.

24 The Denver Art Museum shared digital images of the cards with me when requested. Red Star discusses access to collections here: Taylor Defoe, "Rising Artist Wendy Red Star on Why She's Bringing Lost Native American Histories to Light on Bus Stops in Three U.S. Cities," *Artnet*, August 24, 2022, https://news.artnet.com/art-world/i-am-the-counter-archive-wendy-red-star-on-her-new-public-art-fund-project-which-brings-native-craft-to-bus-shelterss-2164257.

25 See Denene De Quintal, "Illustrations Make Native Arts Catalog Cards Works of Art," Denver Art Museum Blog, April 26, 2017, https://www.denverartmuseum.org/en/blog/illustrations-make-native-arts-catalog-cards-works-art. The art in the card catalog exists beyond the Native Arts collection, and, according to a blog entry written by curatorial fellow De Quintal, some of the paintings were made by museum staff, before the hiring of WPA artists in the 1930s, and this practice continued into the 1970s. De Quintal writes, "Frederic H. Douglas, one of the DAM's preeminent curators, commissioned the WPA workers when the museum was low on funding and many Americans were in need of employment." Red Star encountered them while serving as a Native Arts Artist-in-Residence at the museum in 2016. She talks about the Denver Art Museum here: Abaki Beck, "Decolonizing Photography: A Conversation with Wendy Red Star," *Aperture*, December 14, 2016, https://aperture.org/editorial/wendy-red-star/. Per John Lukavic, the Andrew W. Mellon Curator of Native American Art, the Denver Art Museum purchased all fifteen prints from this series in 2019 with the Nancy Blomberg Acquisition Fund for Native American Art, and in 2024, they added the entire set of the *1880 Delegation* series via a gift from a private collector. Email to author, Jan. 10, 2024.

26 https://www.denverartmuseum.org/en/object/1938.52..

27 See Jane Anderson and Sonya Atalay, "Repatriation as Pedagogy," *Current Anthropology* 64, no. 6 (2023): 670–91; Amy Lonetree, *Decolonizing Museums: Representing Native America in National and Tribal Museums* (University of North Carolina Press, 2012); Susan Sleeper-Smith, "Introduction," in *Contesting Knowledge: Museums and Indigenous Perspectives*, ed. Susan Sleeper-Smith (University of Nebraska Press, 2009), 1-5.

28 The Oxford English Dictionary defines the verb accession: "To record as a new accession to the collection of a library, museum, etc."

29 Defoe, "Rising Artist Wendy Red Star."

30 Thompson, "Wendy Red Star and the Indigenous Voice." Thompson writes, "For Red Star, unexpected colors are simply an extension of the culture she grew up with on the Apsáalooke reservation in Montana. Electric pinks, blues, yellows, reds. 'Colors that don't necessarily go together but somehow work — that's very much part of the Crow palette,' she says."

31 Tanya Lukin Linklater, "The Insistence of a Crow Archivist: Wendy Red Star," *BlackFlash Magazine* 33, no. 2 (2017), https://blackflash.ca/2017/02/03/wendy-red-star/.

32 See Darren Lone Fight's essay in this volume for a discussion of his preference in using the latter.

33 NAGPRA, or the Native American Graves Protection and Repatriation Act (Pub. L. 101-601, 25 U.S.C. 3001 et seq., 104 Stat. 3048), was passed in 1990 and "recognizes the rights of lineal descendants, Indian Tribes, and Native Hawaiian organizations in Native American human remains, funerary objects, sacred objects, and objects of cultural patrimony" and provides a mechanism for the return of ancestors' remains and heritage objects from museums and other institutions that have them in inventory. Revisions were announced on December 13, 2023. Notably, the Smithsonian Institution is exempt from NAGPRA regulations. https://www.federalregister.gov/documents/2023/12/13/2023-27040/native-american-graves-protection-and-repatriation-act-systematic-processes-for-disposition-or.

34 Hannah Turner, *Cataloguing Culture: Legacies of Colonialism in Museum Documentation* (University of British Columbia Press, 2020). Many of the images of the heritage objects on the Denver Art Museum website are photographed with a gray background, thus the yellow background of the card provides more contrast.

35 A hole is visible on some but not all the digital images of the cards, some of which can be seen here: https://www.denverartmuseum.org/en/blog/illustrations-make-native-arts-catalog-cards-works-art. According to Jennie Trujillo, Curatorial Fellow at the museum, the cards are now stored in boxes but perhaps were once in a catalog drawer.

36 While some museum card catalogs attach photographs of objects, very few use hand-painted renditions like these.

37 The Denver Art Museum does welcome tribal members to visit with, have ceremony with, discuss care of, and will assist with NAGPRA requests of heritage objects. See https://www.denverartmuseum.org/en/nagpra. Visiting the museum is not always feasible, however.

38 This series was a special project for *Aperture*. The images appear in *Wendy Red Star: Delegation*, 60-67. Red Star says that *Bíiluuke* means "I'm Crow and this is our side." See Chuck Thompson, "Wendy Red Star and the Indigenous Voice."

39 In the introduction to *Sensible Objects*, Elizabeth Edwards, Chris Gosden, and Ruth B. Phillips write, "The practices [conservators] enforce isolate objects from contact with food (to prevent insect infestation), touch (to prevent breakage and the contamination of skin oils), and changes of temperature or humidity (through the isolation of the artifact in a glass case or closed storage area)." See Elizabeth Edwards, Chris Gosden, and Ruth B. Phillips, "Introduction," in *Sensible Objects: Colonialism, Museums, and Material Culture* (Berg, 2006), 20.

40 Julia Bryan-Wilson, "Wendy Red Star: Crow Hands, Crow Objects," Special Issue: *Native America*, *Aperture* 240 (Fall 2020), 130. Bryan-Wilson writes, "She frequently draws on the photographs she creates, treating the print like a skin to be embellished, tattooed, and marked; she also plumbs archives around Native histories as she explores how her own body interacts with places both real and imagined."

41 Constance Classen and David Howes, "The Museum as Sensescape: Western Sensibilities and Indigenous Artifacts," in *Sensible Objects: Colonialism, Museums, and Material Culture*, eds. Elizabeth Edwards, Chris Gosden, and Ruth B. Phillips (Berg, 2006), 202. Classen and Howes write, "[T]ouch functioned as an important medium of intimacy between the visitor to the collection and the collection itself. Through touch the visitor and the collection are united, physically joined together."

42 Tanya Lukin Linklater, "'We Wear One Another,'" *Journal of Visual Culture* 21, no. 1 (2022): 89.

43 In the introduction to *Sensible Objects*, Edwards, Gosden, and Phillips explain, "Today, standard museum protocols are increasingly being challenged by members of the communities from which the objects originate. They argue that the Western museum's ritual practices of sensory isolation and enforced stasis are antithetical to Indigenous forms of ritual correctness that may require that objects be fed, held, worn, played, danced, or exposed to air, water, or incense." Edwards, et al, *Sensible Objects*, 20. In a conversation between Red Star and Emily Moazami of NMAI, the two talk about traditional care of heritage items; see Wendy Red Star, "People of the Earth," 23-31.

44 Jacki Rand points out that "traditional care and handling" allows for and encourages use of belongings held in museums. See Jacki Rand, "Why I Can't Visit the National Museum of the American Indian: Reflections of an Accidental Privileged Insider, 1989-1994," *Common-Place* 7, no. 4 (2007), https://common-place.online/article/why-i-cant-visit-the-national-museum-of-the-american-indian/.

45 See Red Star, *Wendy Red Star: Delegation*, 60.

46 See Red Star, *Wendy Red Star: Delegation*, 62.

47 See Red Star, *Wendy Red Star: Delegation*, 64-65.

48 LeAnne Howe, "The Story of America: A Tribalography," in *Clearing a Path: Theorizing the Past in Native American Studies*, ed. Nancy Shoemaker (Routledge, 2002), 29-48.

49 All the collages are titled in this way, Apsáalooke word (English translation). All except one are named for the objects [the one that isn't is called *akashappéelilia (camp crier)*].

50 This collage is the only one with red ink. The rest have text in black or brown ink.

51 See https://americanindian.si.edu/collections-search/object/NMAI_220543.

52 Defoe, "Rising Artist Wendy Red Star."

PLATES

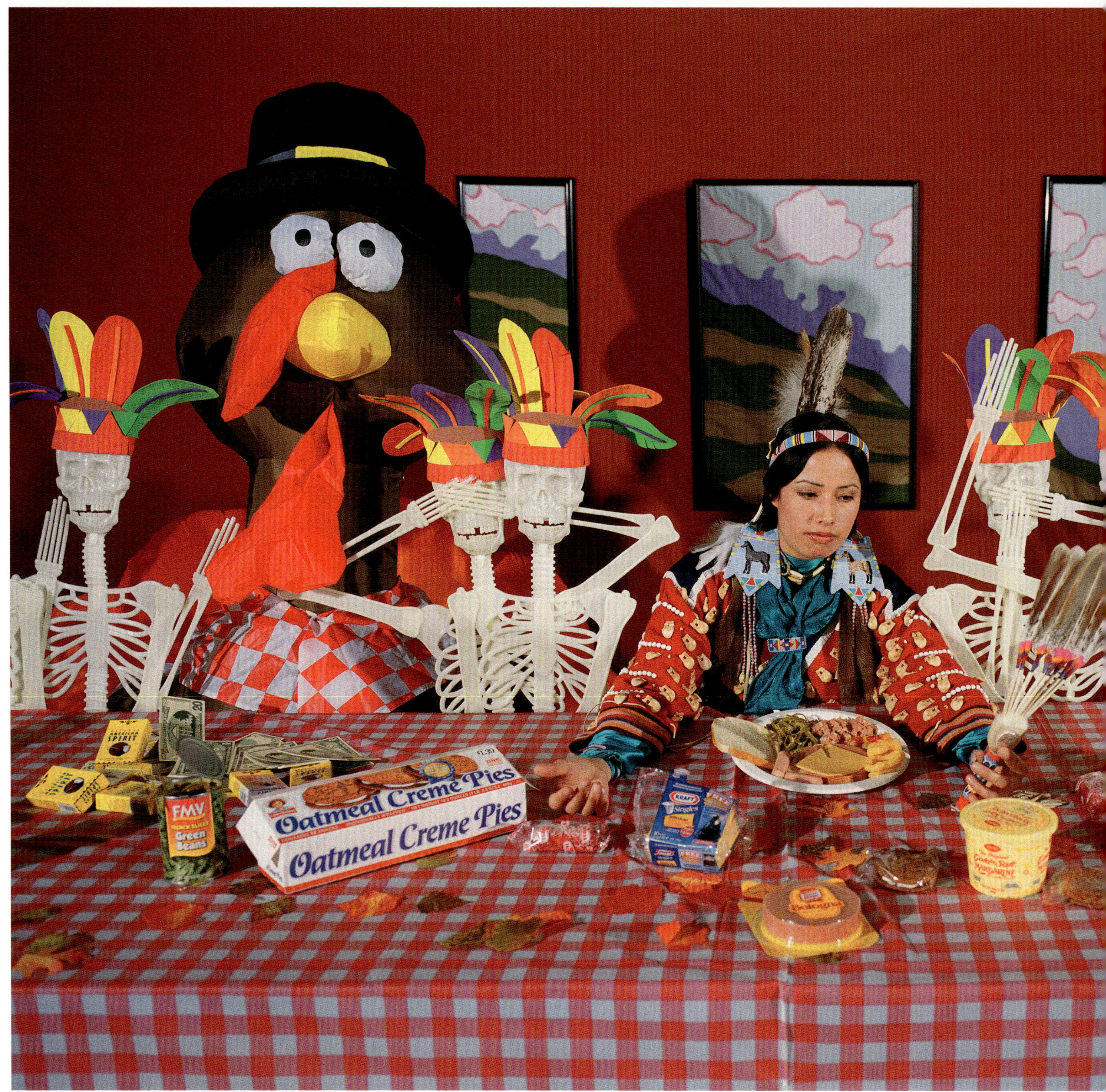

AMERICAN SPIRIT
FMV
FRENCH SLICES
Green Beans
Oatmeal Creme Pies
CONTAINS 12 SINDIVIDUAL
Oatmeal Creme Pies
KRAFT
Singles
Bologna

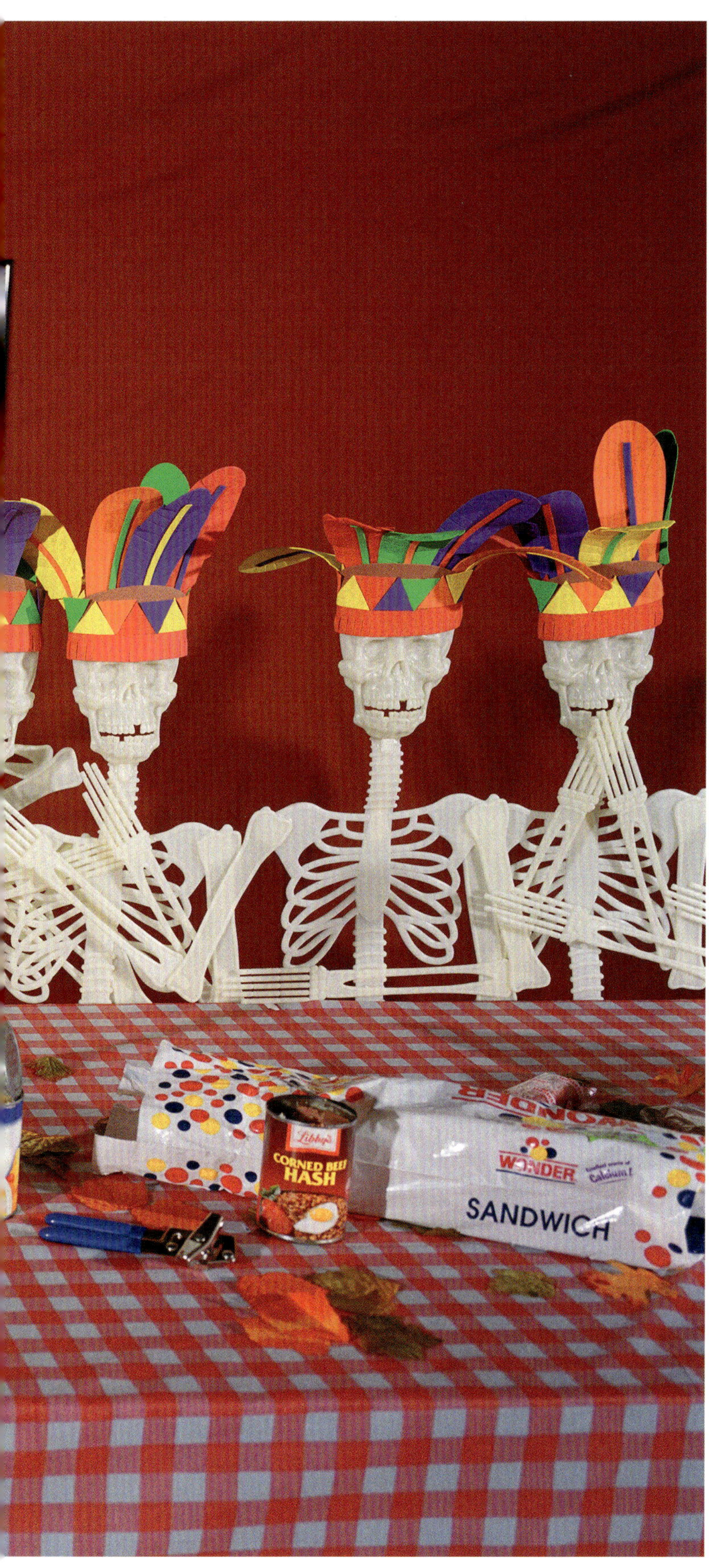

The Last Thanks

2006

Archival pigment print

24 x 36 in. (61 x 91.4 cm)

Courtesy Forge Project Collection, traditional lands of the Moh-He-Con-Nuck

Image courtesy of the artist and Sargent's Daughters © Wendy Red Star

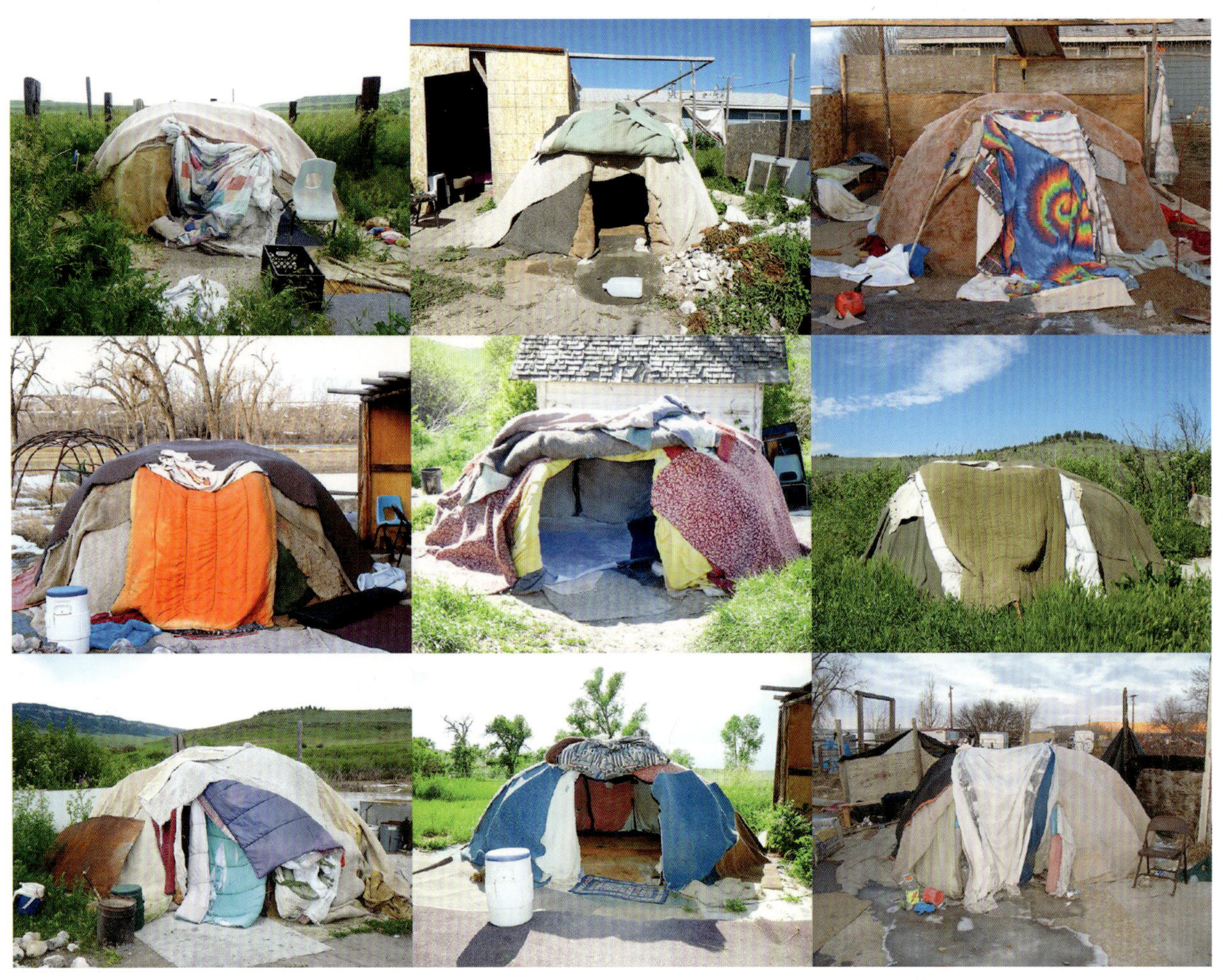

My Home is Where My Tipi Sits
(Sweat Lodges)

2011

Archival pigment print

57 x 72 in. (144.78 x 182.88 cm)

Courtesy Forge Project Collection,
traditional lands of the Moh-He-
Con-Nuck

© Wendy Red Star

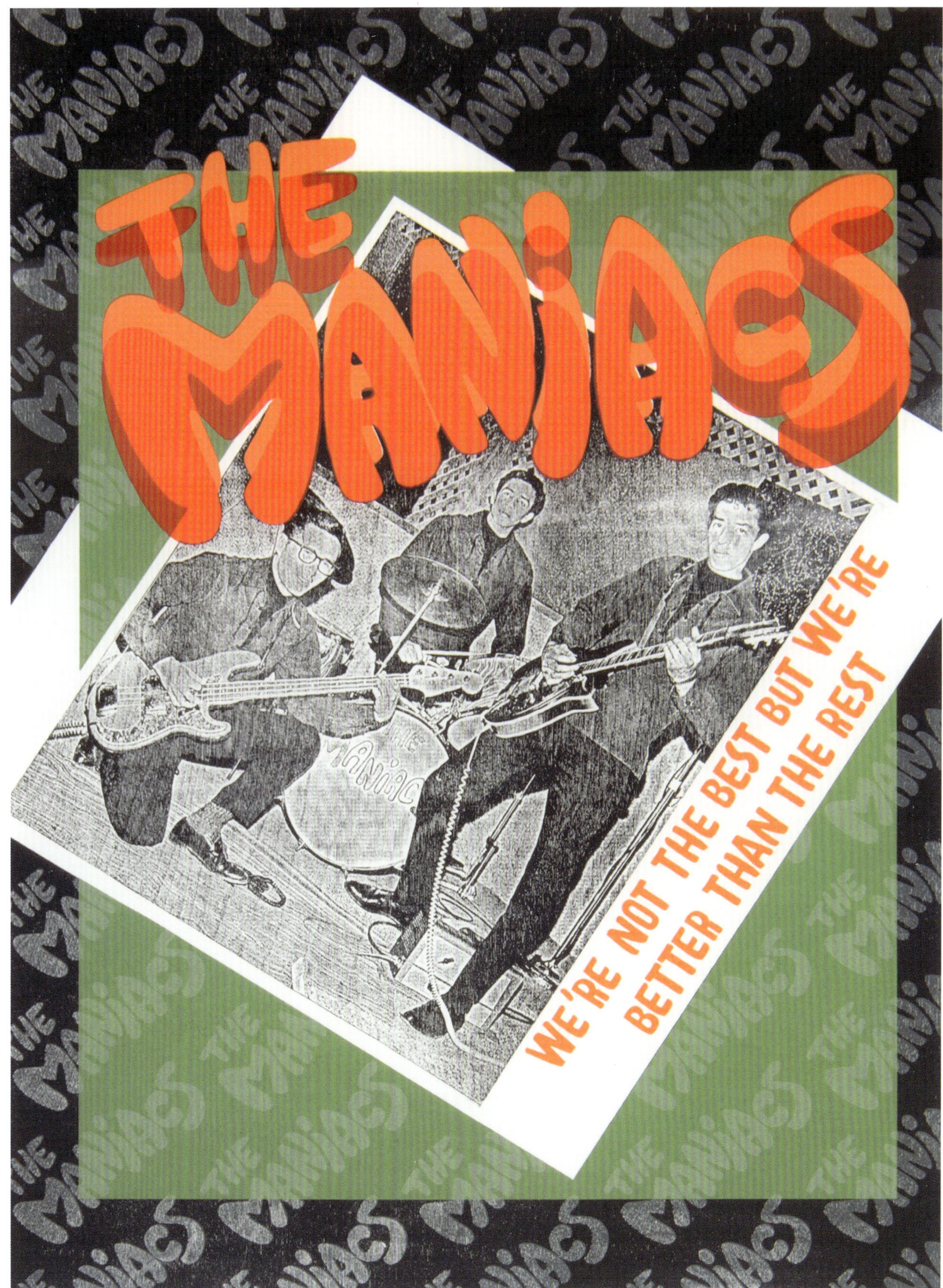

The Maniacs

2018

Lithograph and screenprint

27 x 19 in. (68.58 x 48.26 cm)

Image courtesy of the artist and Sargent's Daughters © Wendy Red Star

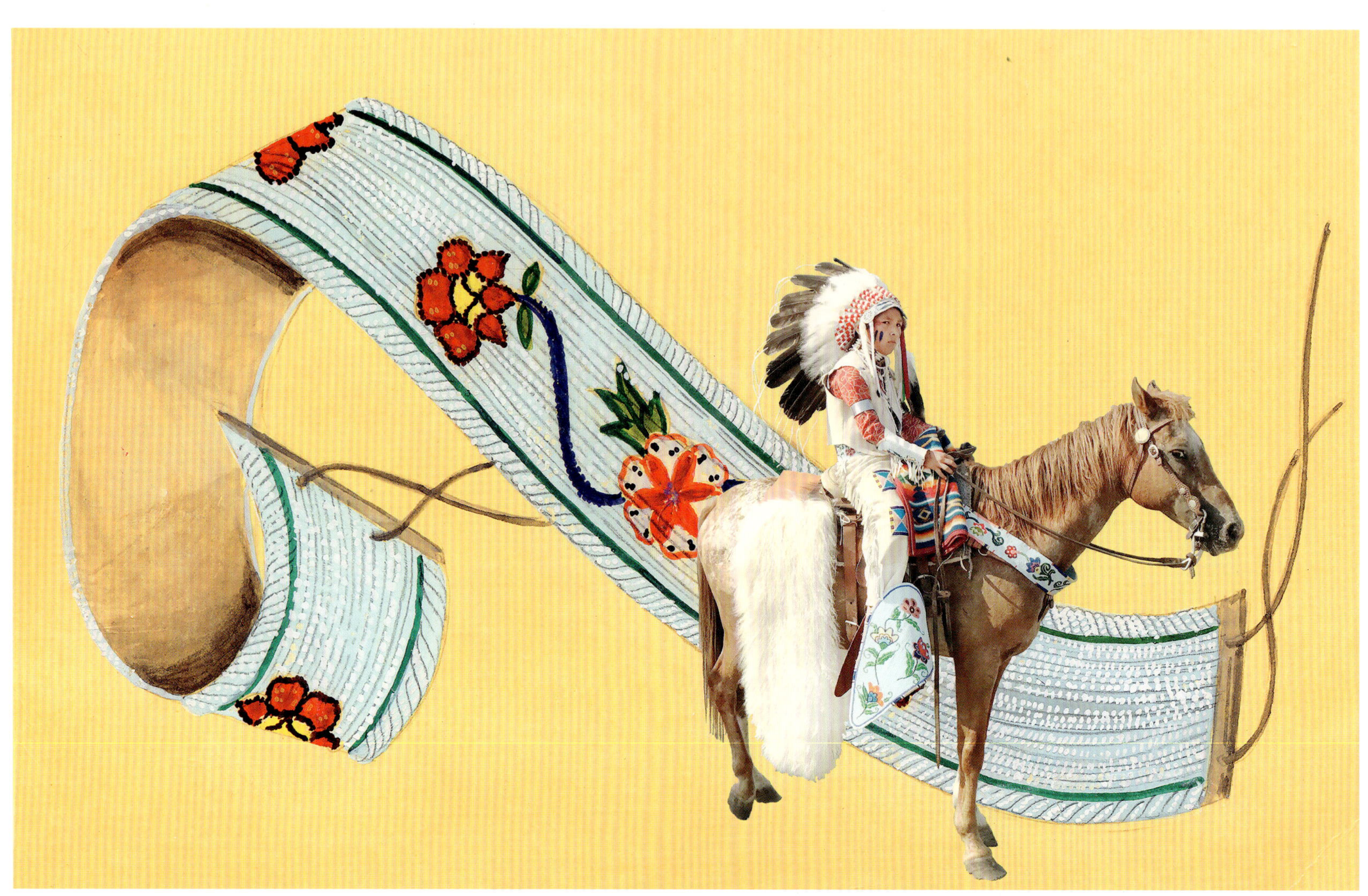

Catalogue Number 1949.72

2019

Pigment print on archival paper,
edition 1 of 10 and 2 AP

28 x 18 in. (71.1 x 45.7 cm)

Image courtesy of the artist and
Sargent's Daughters © Wendy Red Star

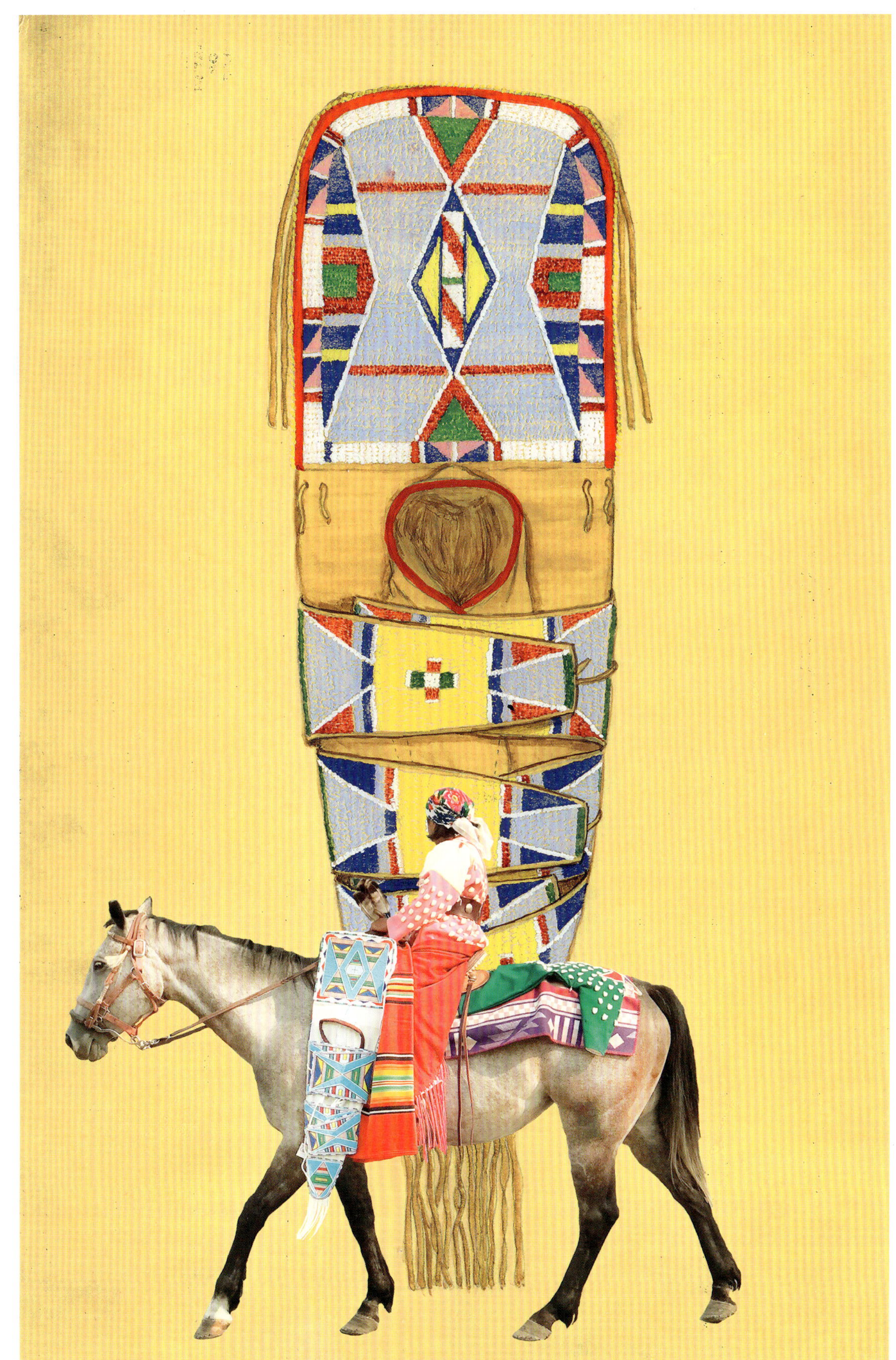

Catalogue Number 1938.52

2019

Pigment print on archival paper,
edition 1 of 10 and 2 AP

28 x 18 in. (71.1 x 45.7 cm)

Image courtesy of the artist and
Sargent's Daughters © Wendy Red Star

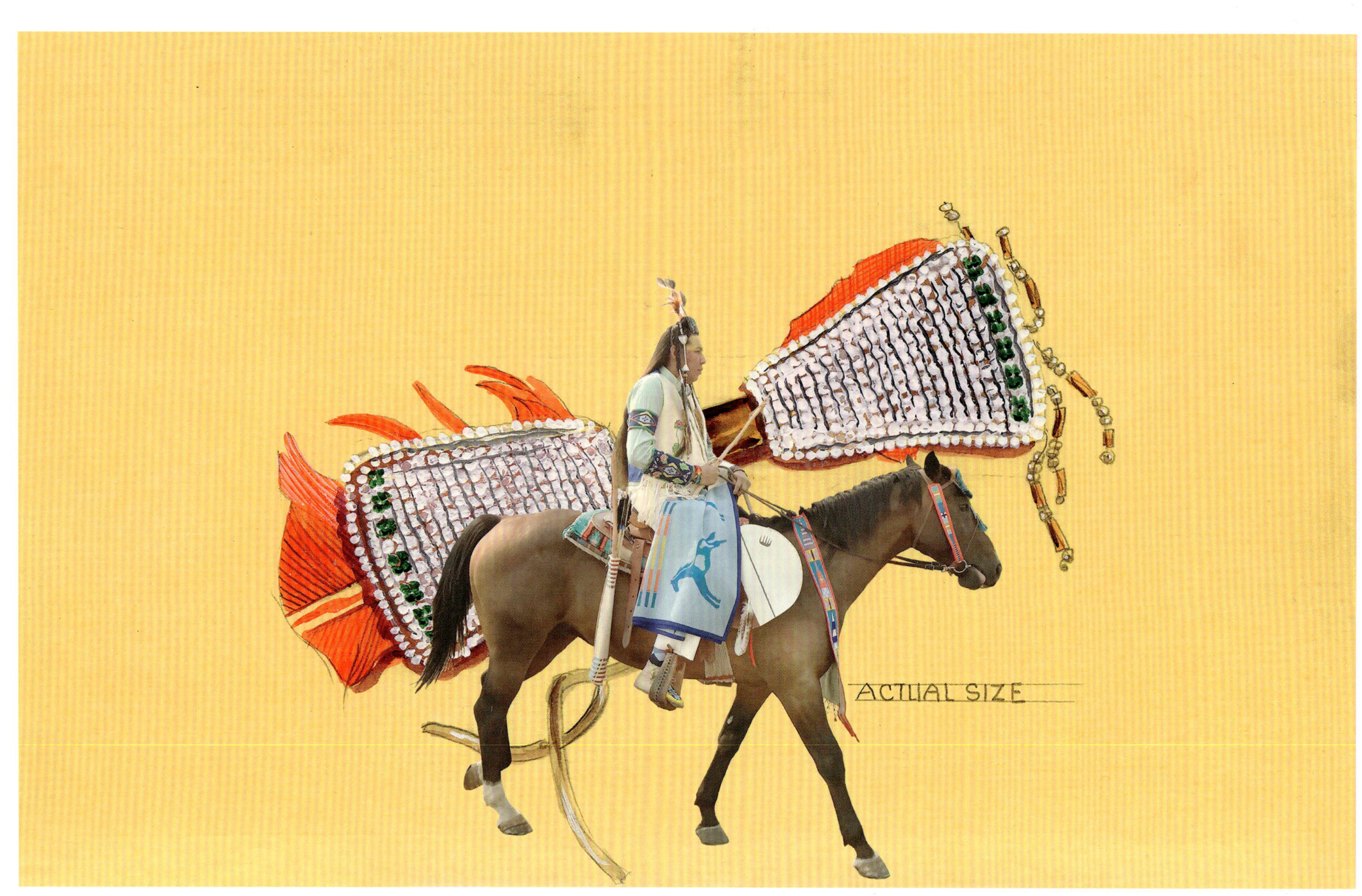

Catalogue Number 1941.30.1

2019

Pigment print on archival paper,
edition 1 of 10 and 2 AP

28 x 18 in. (71.1 x 45.7 cm)

Image courtesy of the artist and
Sargent's Daughters © Wendy Red Star

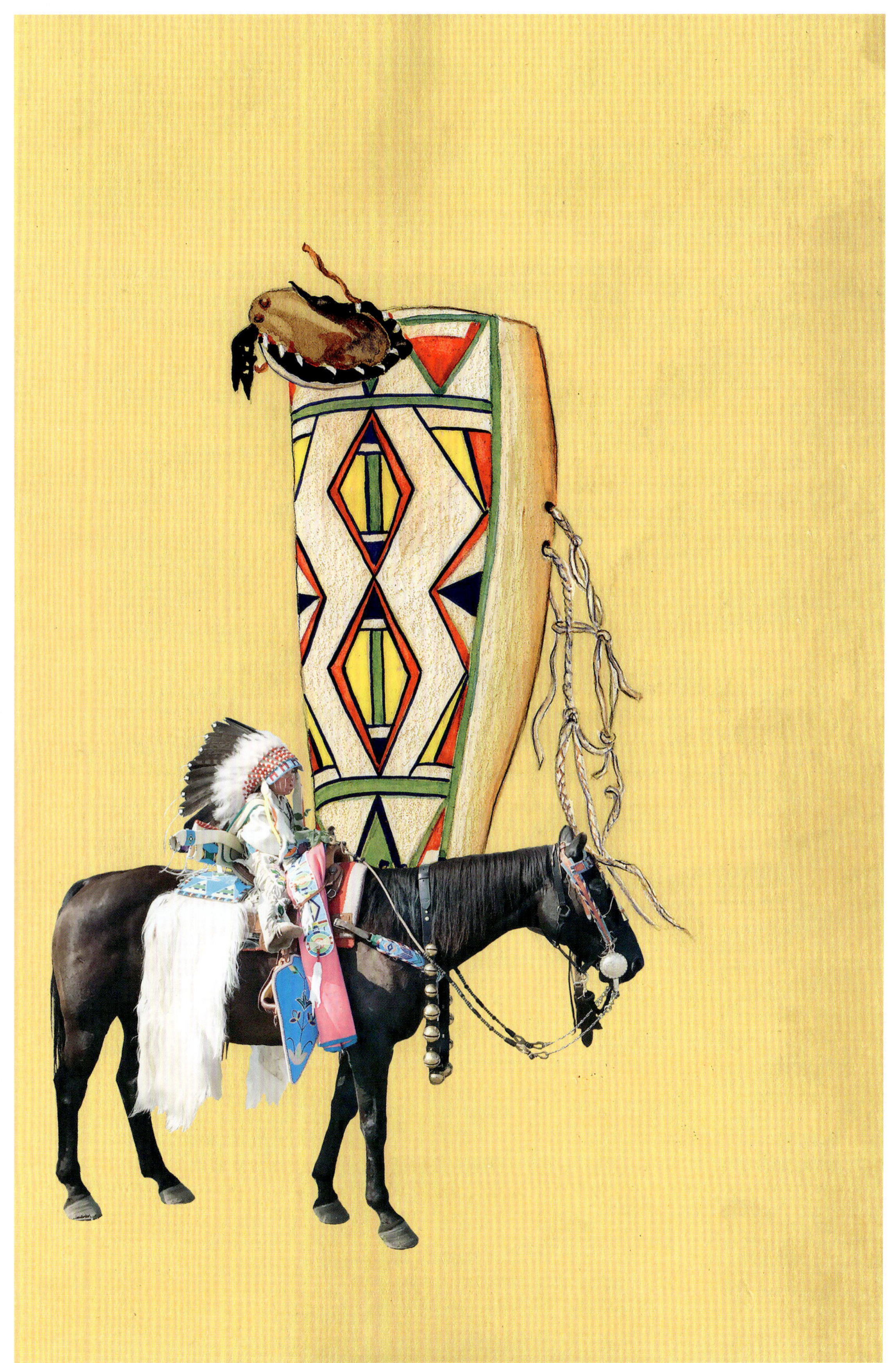

Catalogue Number 1946.82.1

2019

Pigment print on archival paper,
edition 1 of 10 and 2 AP

28 x 18 in. (71.1 x 45.7 cm)

Image courtesy of the artist and
Sargent's Daughters © Wendy Red Star

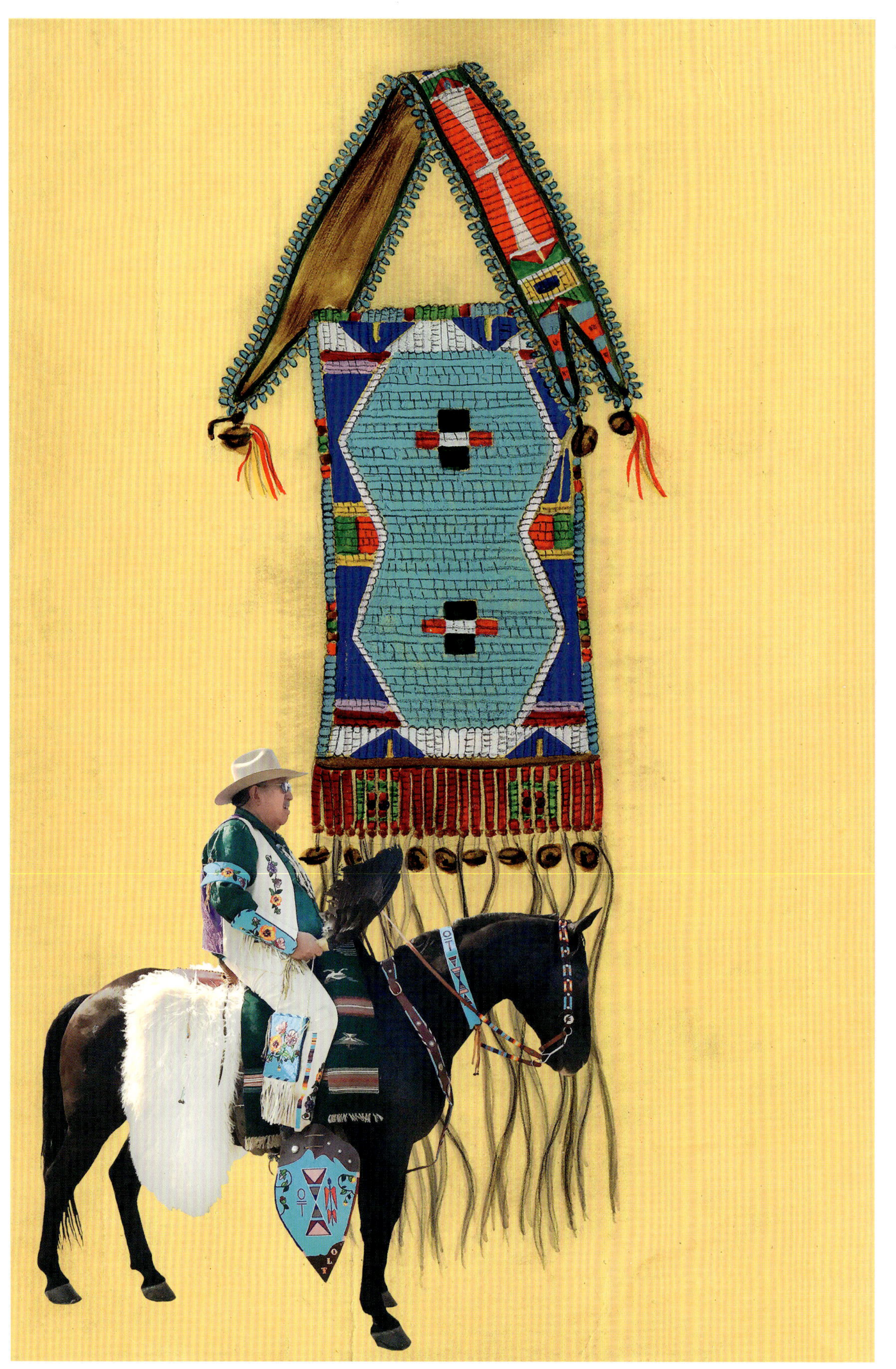

Catalogue Number 1949.66

2019

Pigment print on archival paper,
edition 1 of 10 and 2 AP

28 x 18 in. (71.1 x 45.7 cm)

Image courtesy of the artist and
Sargent's Daughters © Wendy Red Star

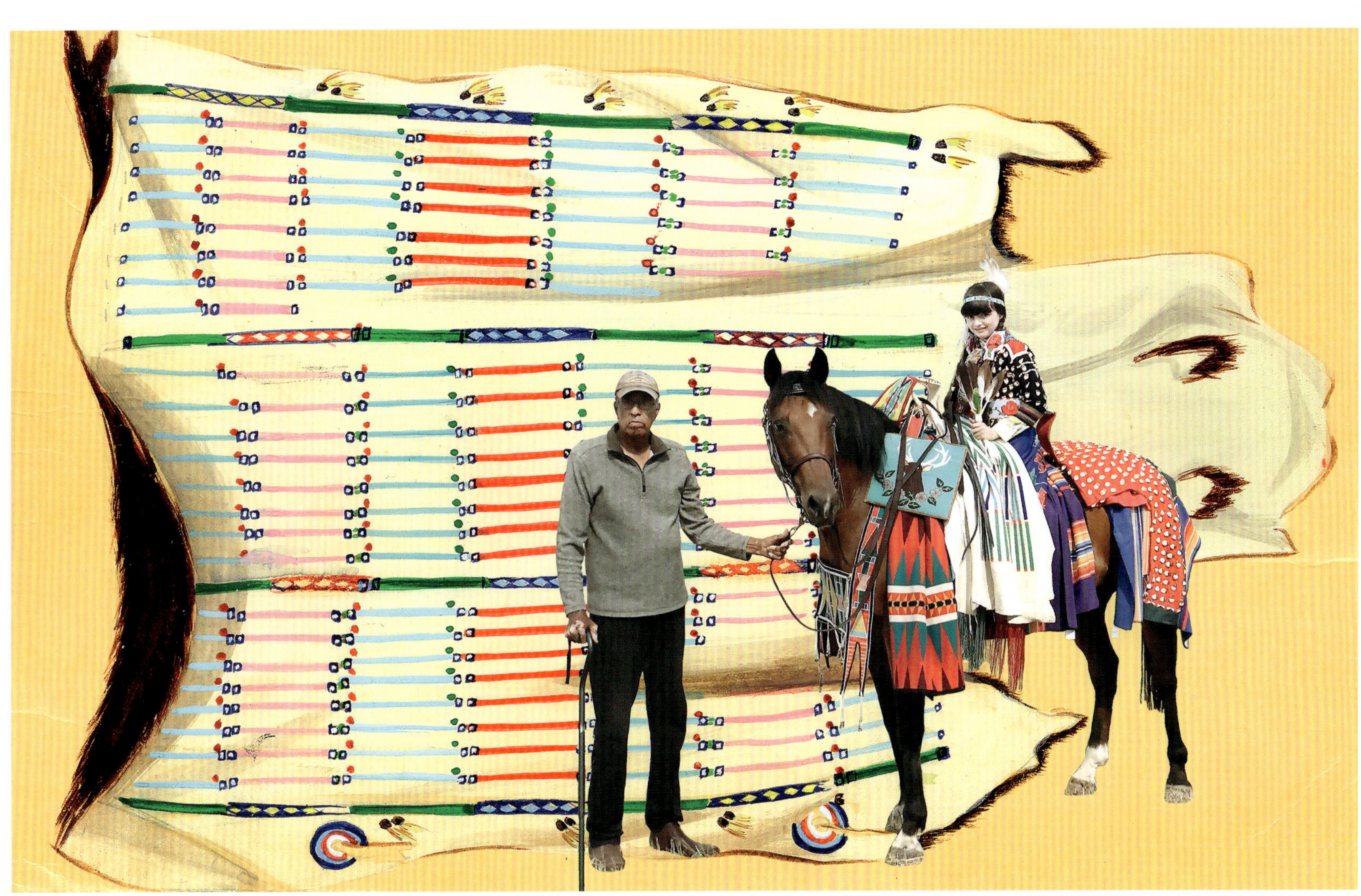

Catalogue Number 1949.73

2019

Pigment print on archival paper,
edition 1 of 10 and 2 AP

28 x 18 in. (71.1 x 45.7 cm)

Image courtesy of the artist and
Sargent's Daughters © Wendy Red Star

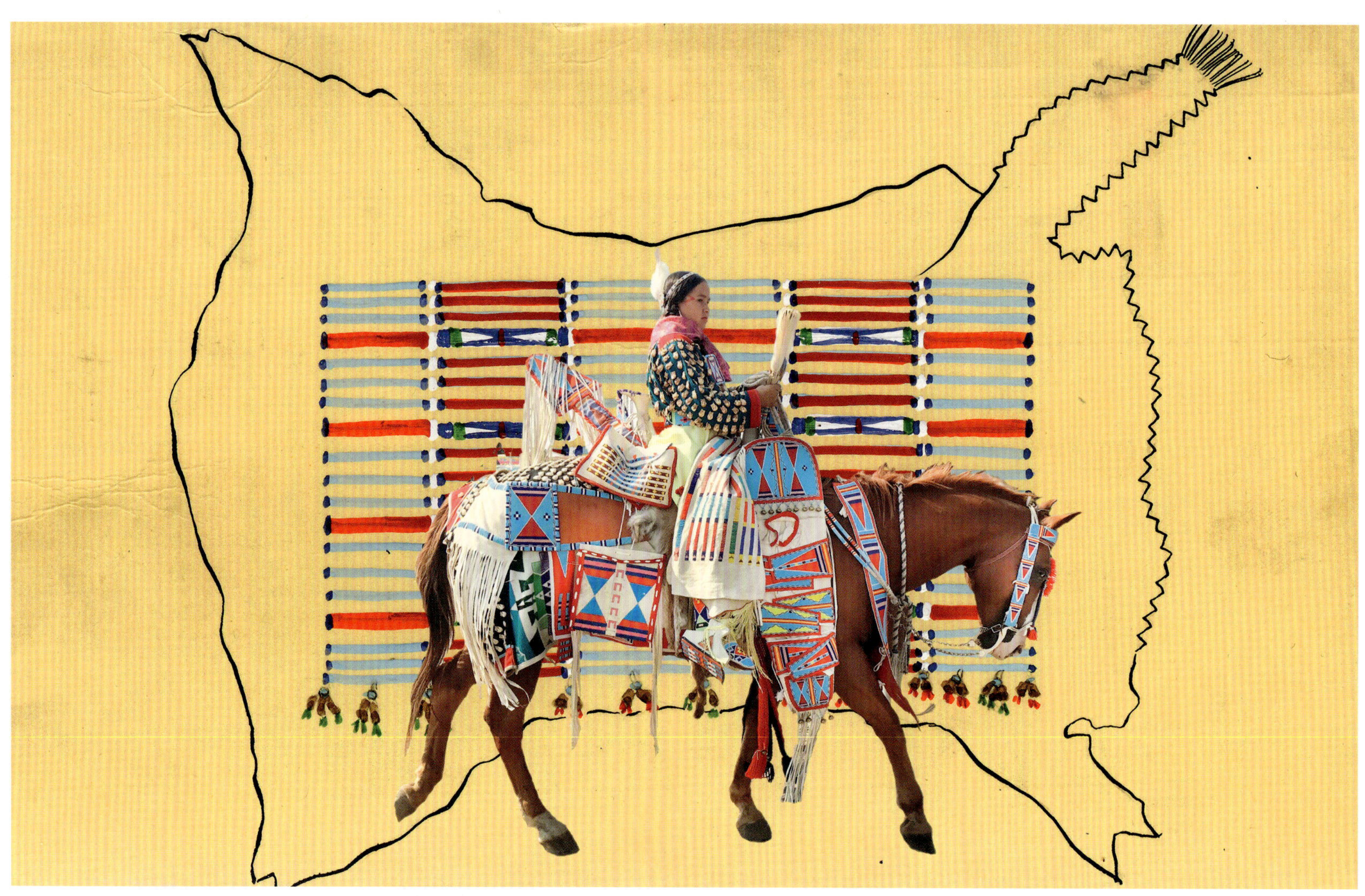

Catalogue Number 1948.102

2019

Pigment print on archival paper,
edition 1 of 10 and 2 AP

18 x 28 in. (45.7 cm x 71.1 cm)

Image courtesy of the artist and
Sargent's Daughters © Wendy Red Star

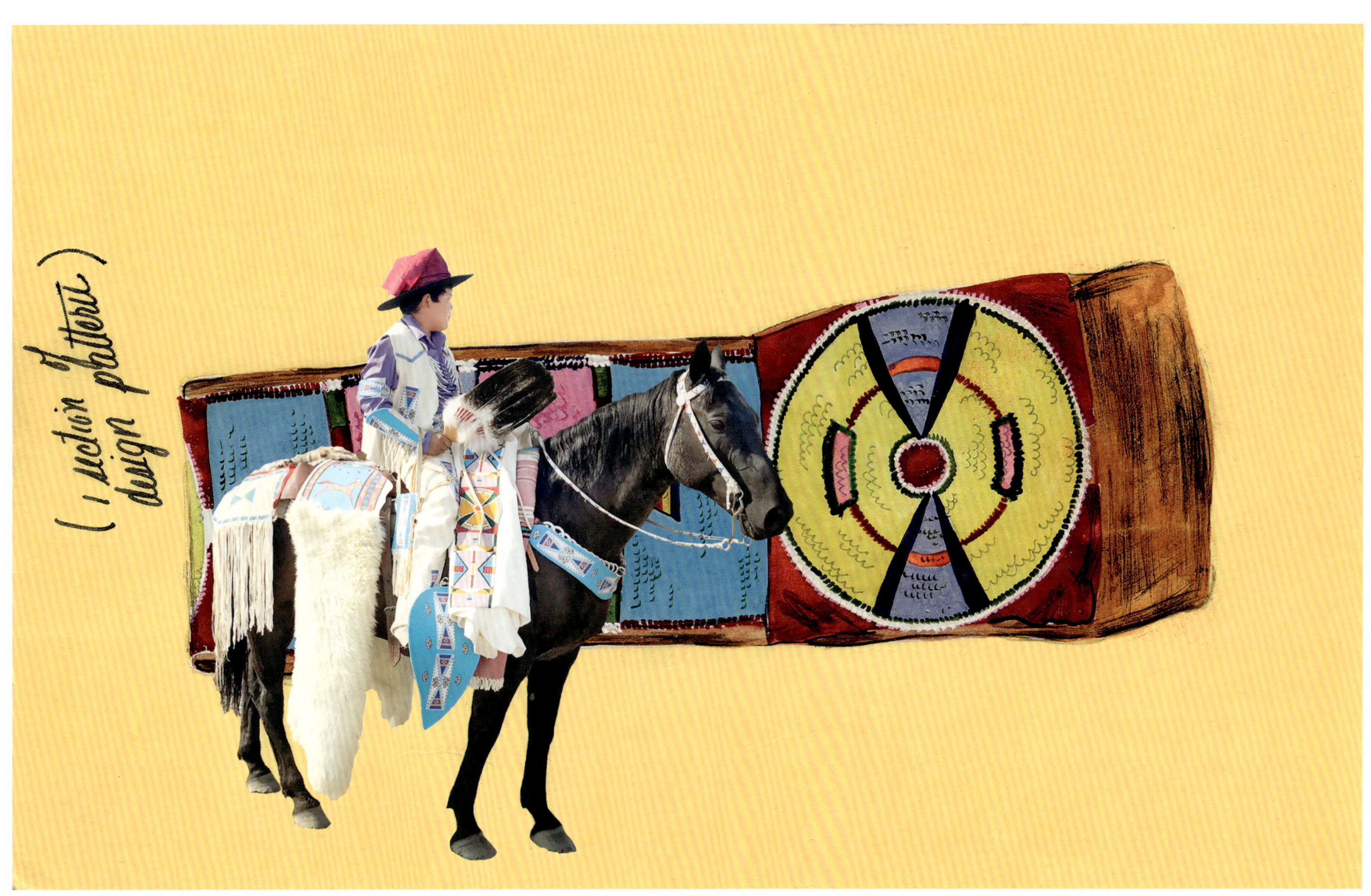

Catalogue Number 1950.74

2019

Pigment print on archival paper,
edition 1 of 10 and 2 AP

18 x 28 in. (45.7 cm x 71.1 cm)

Image courtesy of the artist and
Sargent's Daughters © Wendy Red Star

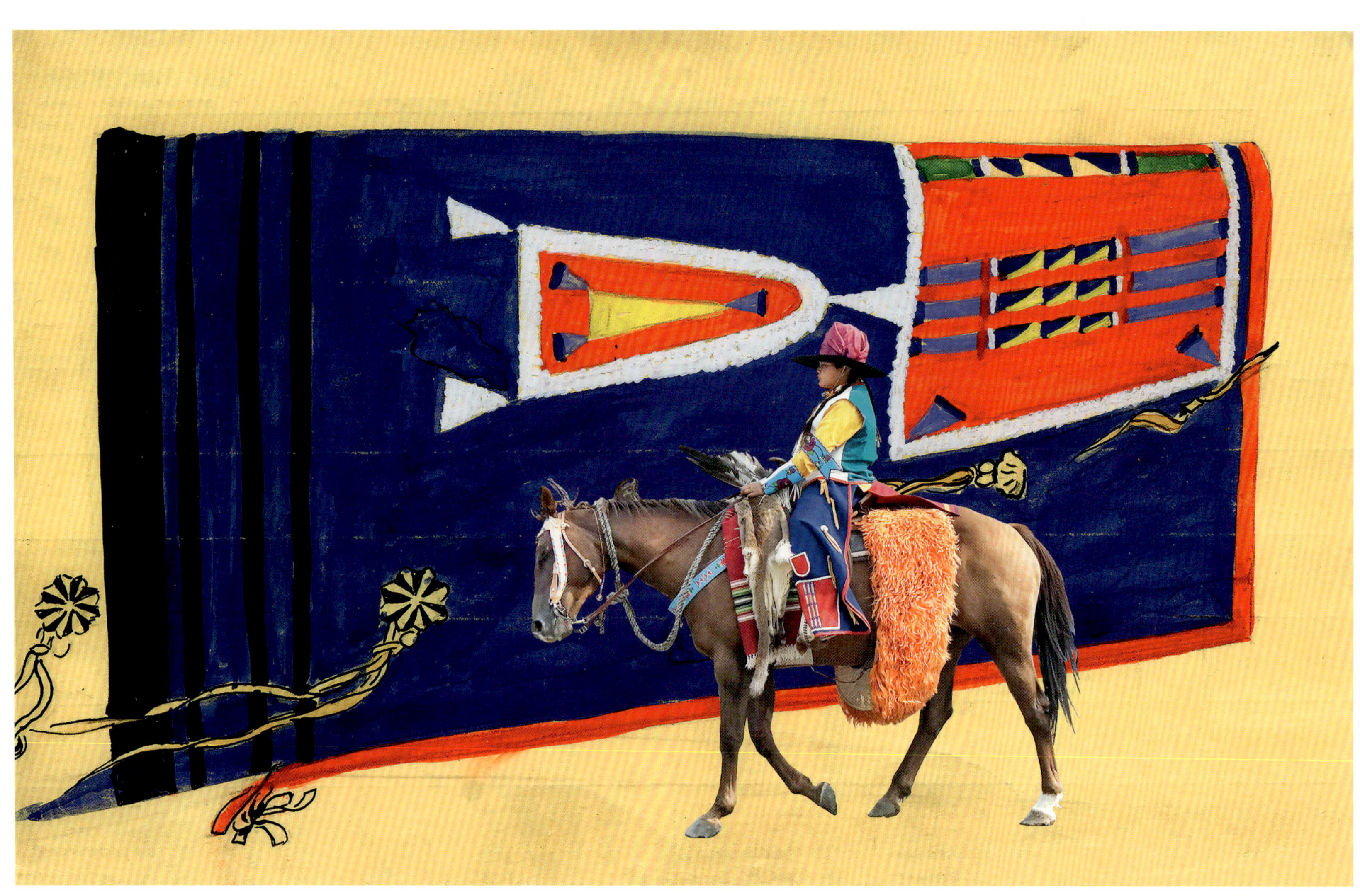

Catalogue Number 1935.33.a,b.

2019

Pigment print on archival paper,
edition 1 of 10 and 2 AP

18 x 28 in. (45.7 cm x 71.1 cm)

Image courtesy of the artist and
Sargent's Daughters © Wendy Red Star

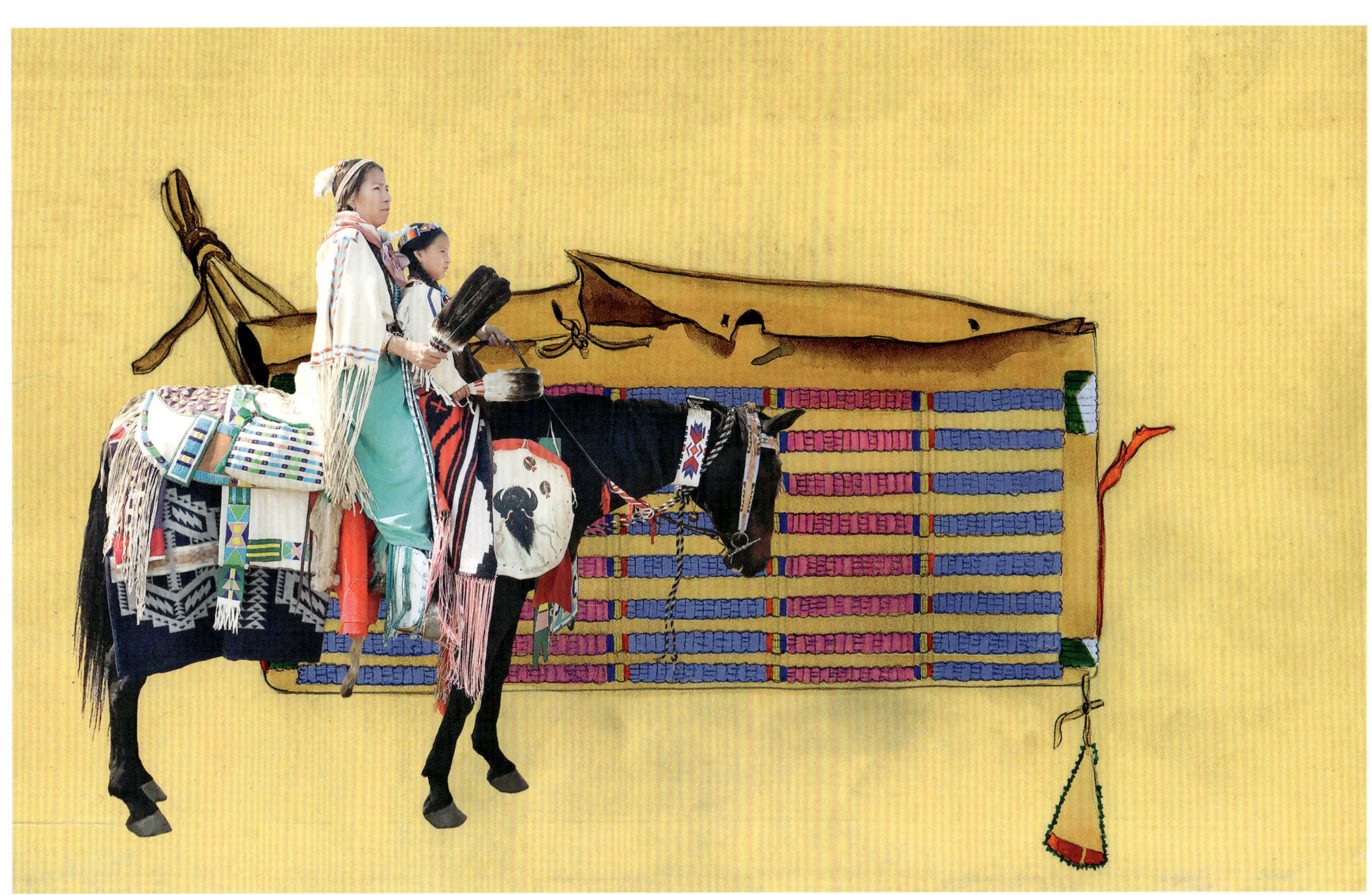

Catalogue Number 1944.26

2019

Pigment print on archival paper,
edition 1 of 10 and 2 AP

18 x 28 in. (45.7 cm x 71.1 cm)

Image courtesy of the artist and
Sargent's Daughters © Wendy Red Star

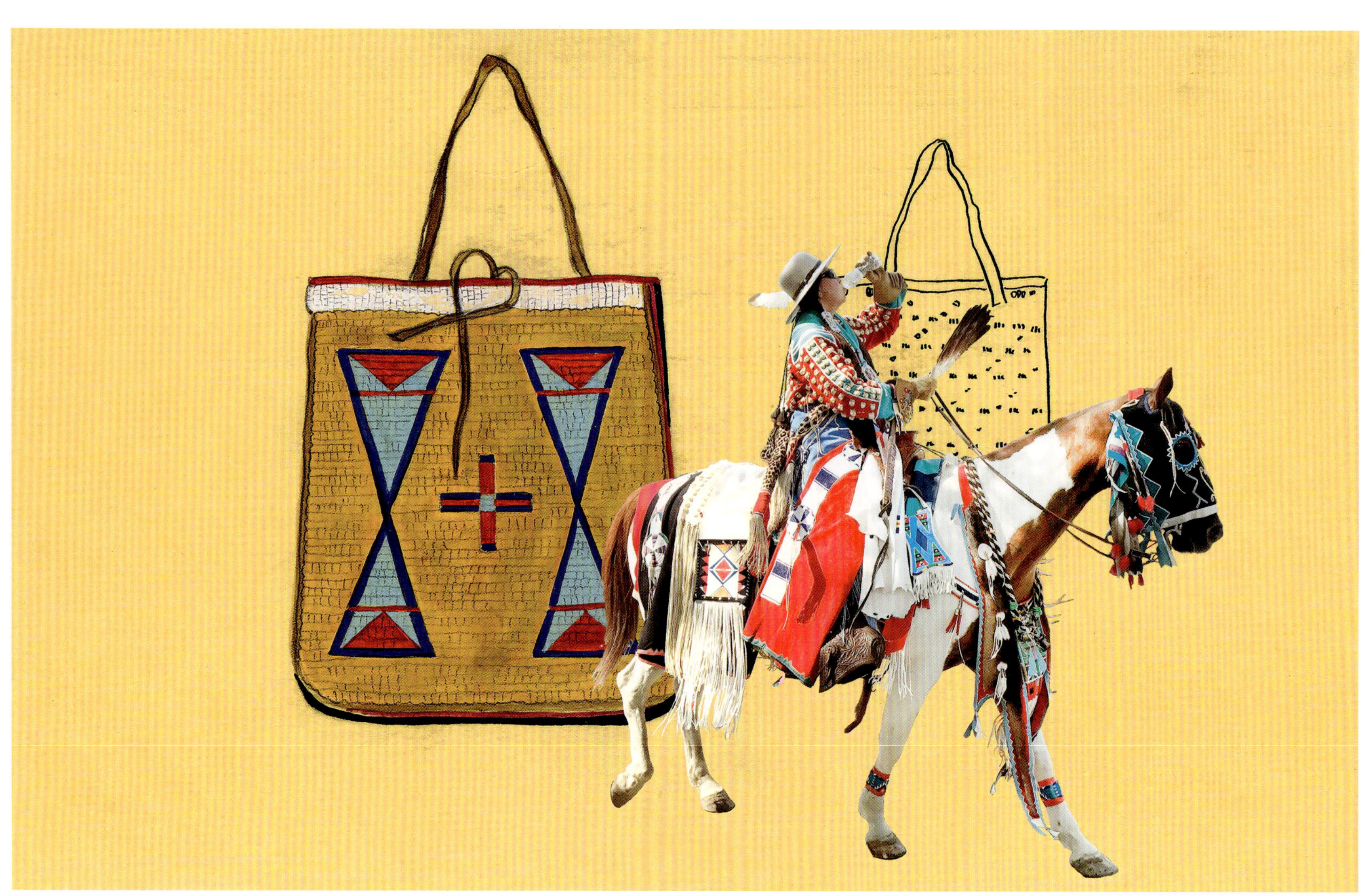

Catalogue Number 1947.110

2019

Pigment print on archival paper,
edition 1 of 10 and 2 AP

18 x 28 in. (45.7 cm x 71.1 cm)

Image courtesy of the artist and
Sargent's Daughters © Wendy Red Star

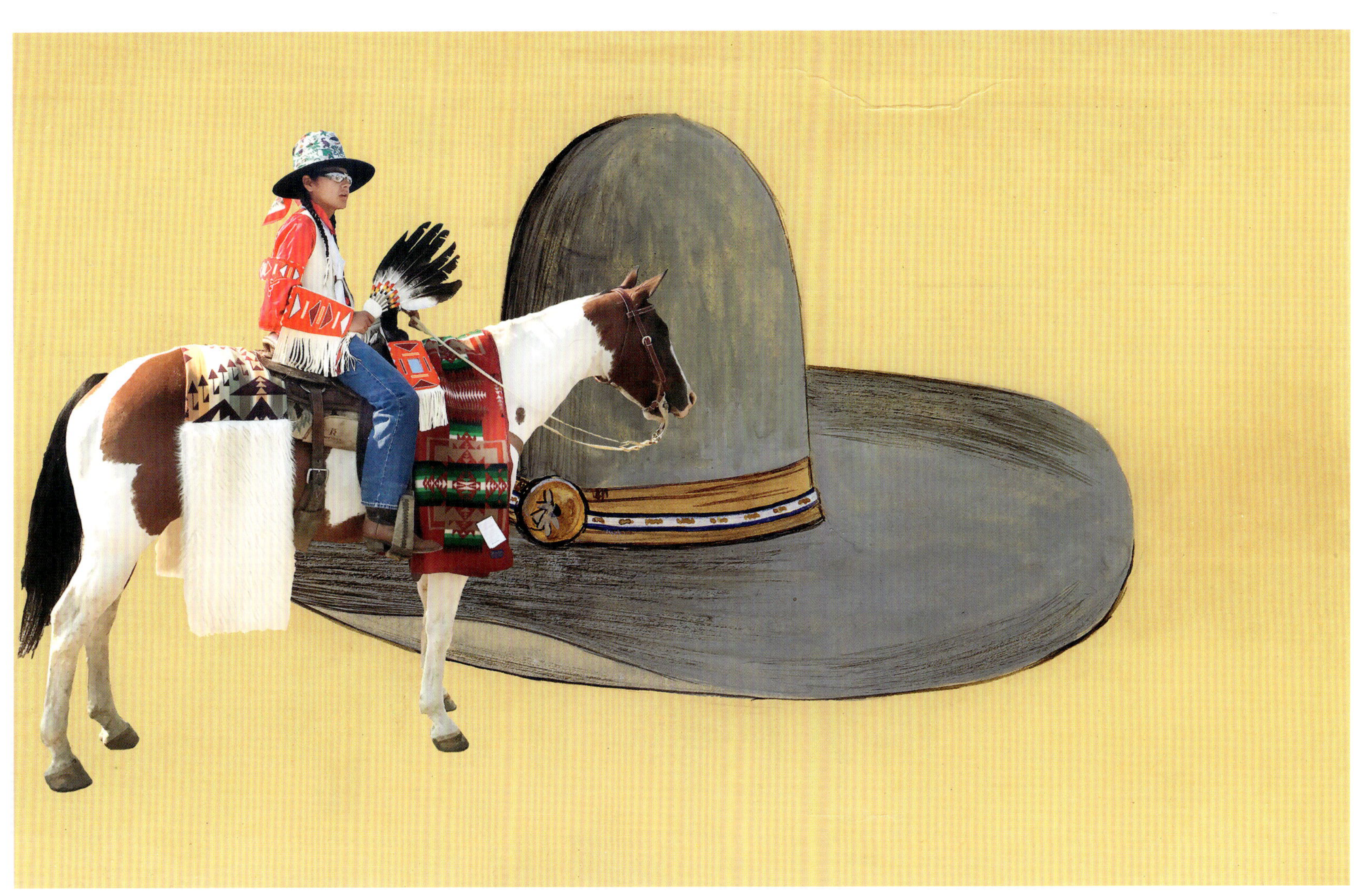

Catalogue Number 1949.105

2019

Pigment print on archival paper,
edition 1 of 10 and 2 AP

18 x 28 in. (45.7 cm x 71.1 cm)

Image courtesy of the artist and
Sargent's Daughters © Wendy Red Star

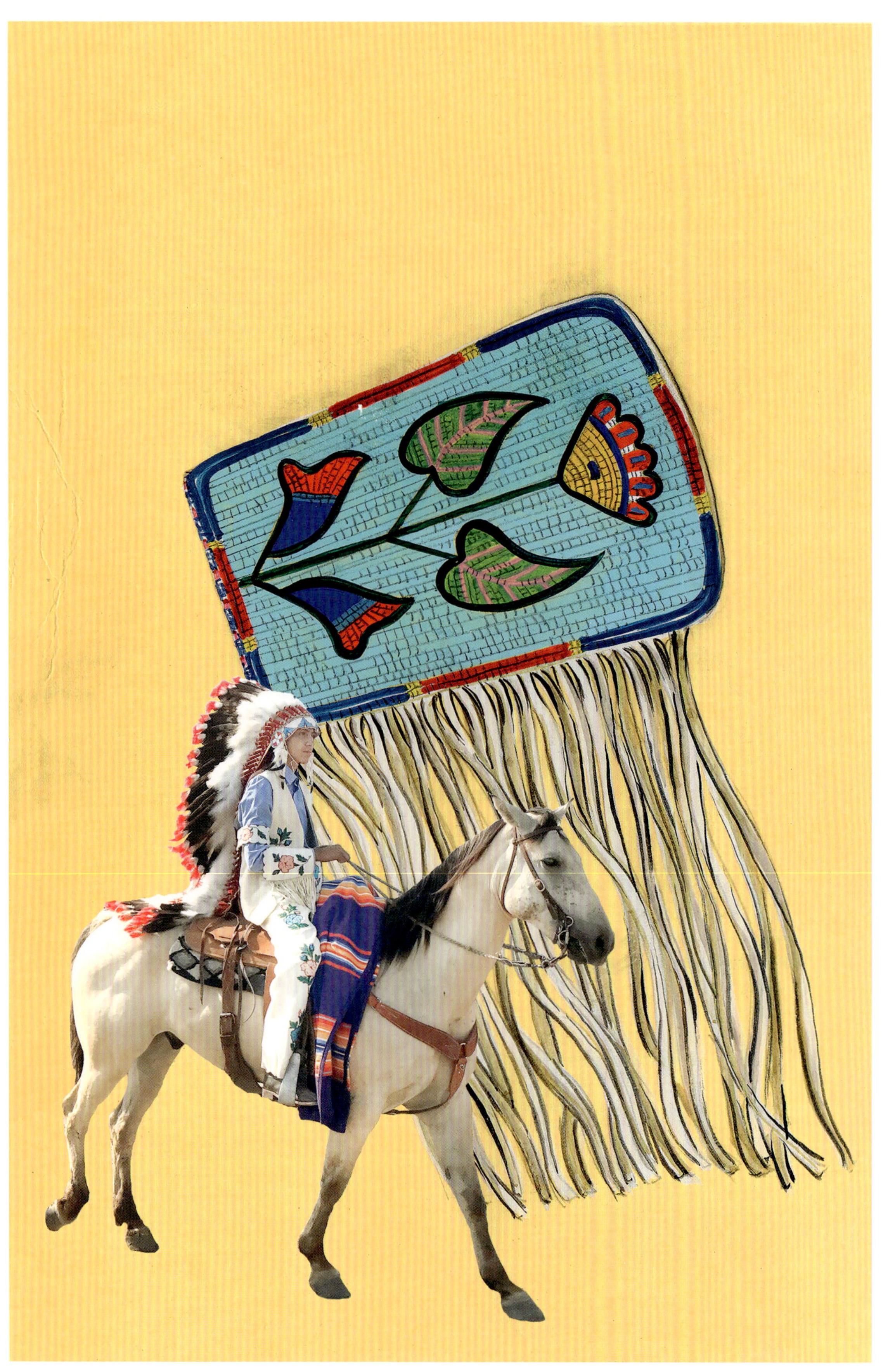

Catalogue Number 1949.67.a,b.
2019
Pigment print on archival paper,
edition 1 of 10 and 2 AP
28 x 18 in. (71.1 x 45.7 cm)
Image courtesy of the artist and
Sargent's Daughters © Wendy Red Star

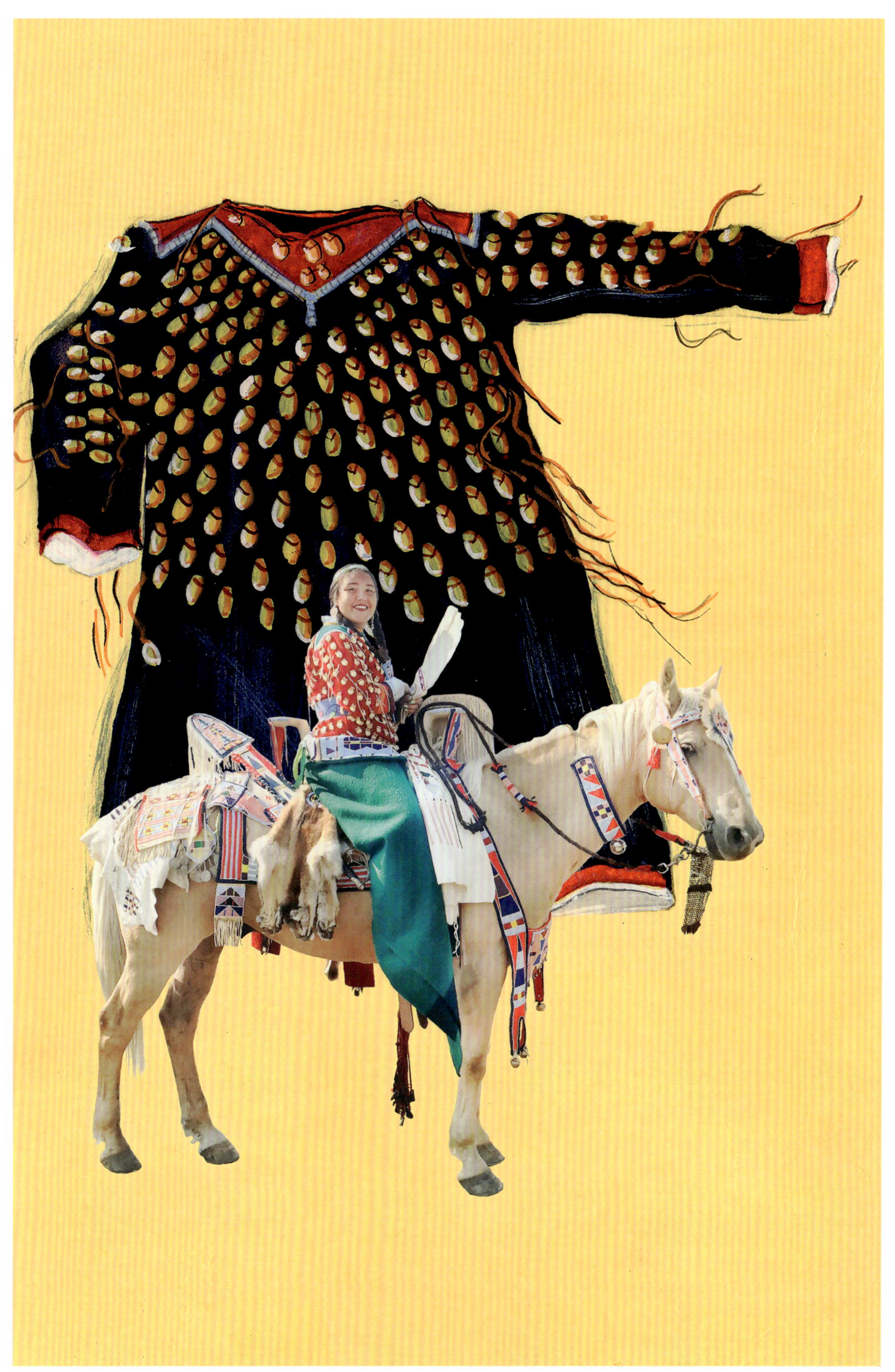

Catalogue Number 1950.76

2019

Pigment print on archival paper,
edition 1 of 10 and 2 AP

28 x 18 in. (71.1 x 45.7 cm)

Image courtesy of the artist and
Sargent's Daughters © Wendy Red Star

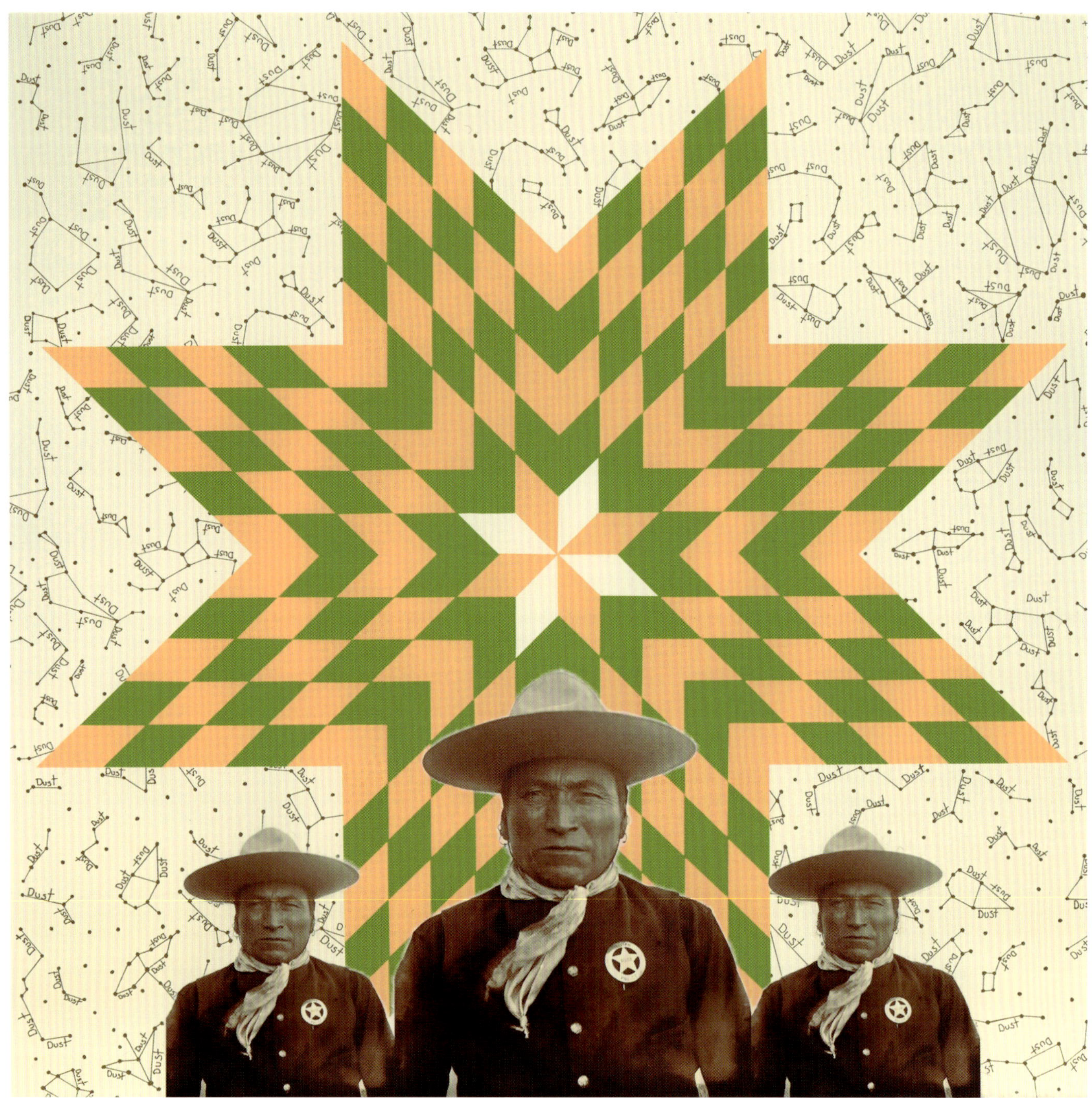

Dust

2021

Three-color lithograph on Somerset
Satin soft white, with archival pigment
printed chine collé on mulberry paper,
edition 15 of 25

20.25 x 20 in. (51.44 x 50.8 cm)

Image courtesy of the artist and
Sargent's Daughters © Wendy Red Star

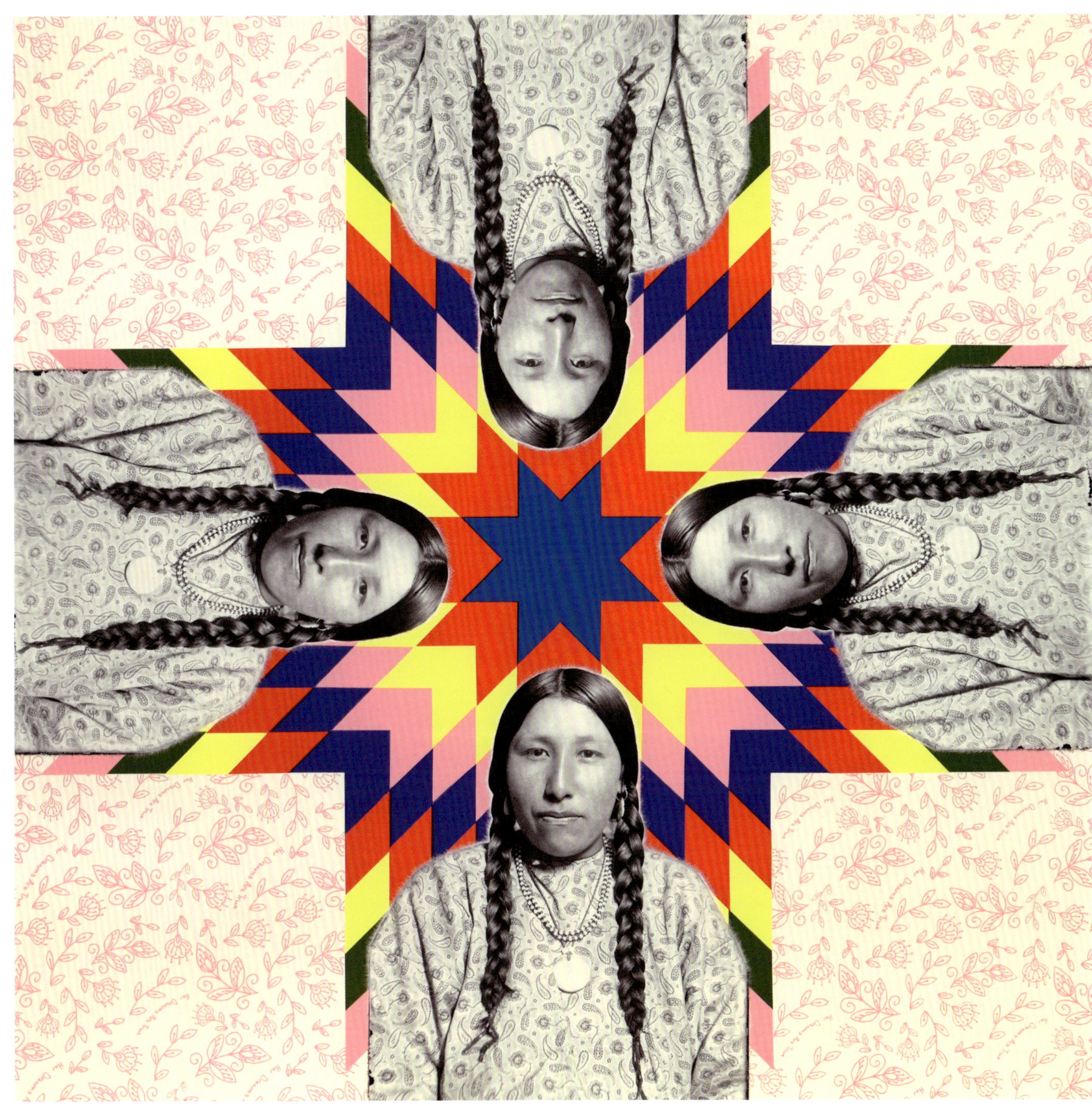

Her Dreams Are True (Julia Bad Boy)

2021

Six-color lithograph on Somerset
Satin soft white, with archival pigment
printed chine collé on mulberry paper,
edition 15 of 25

20.25 x 20 in. (51.44 x 50.8 cm)

Image courtesy of the artist and
Sargent's Daughters © Wendy Red Star

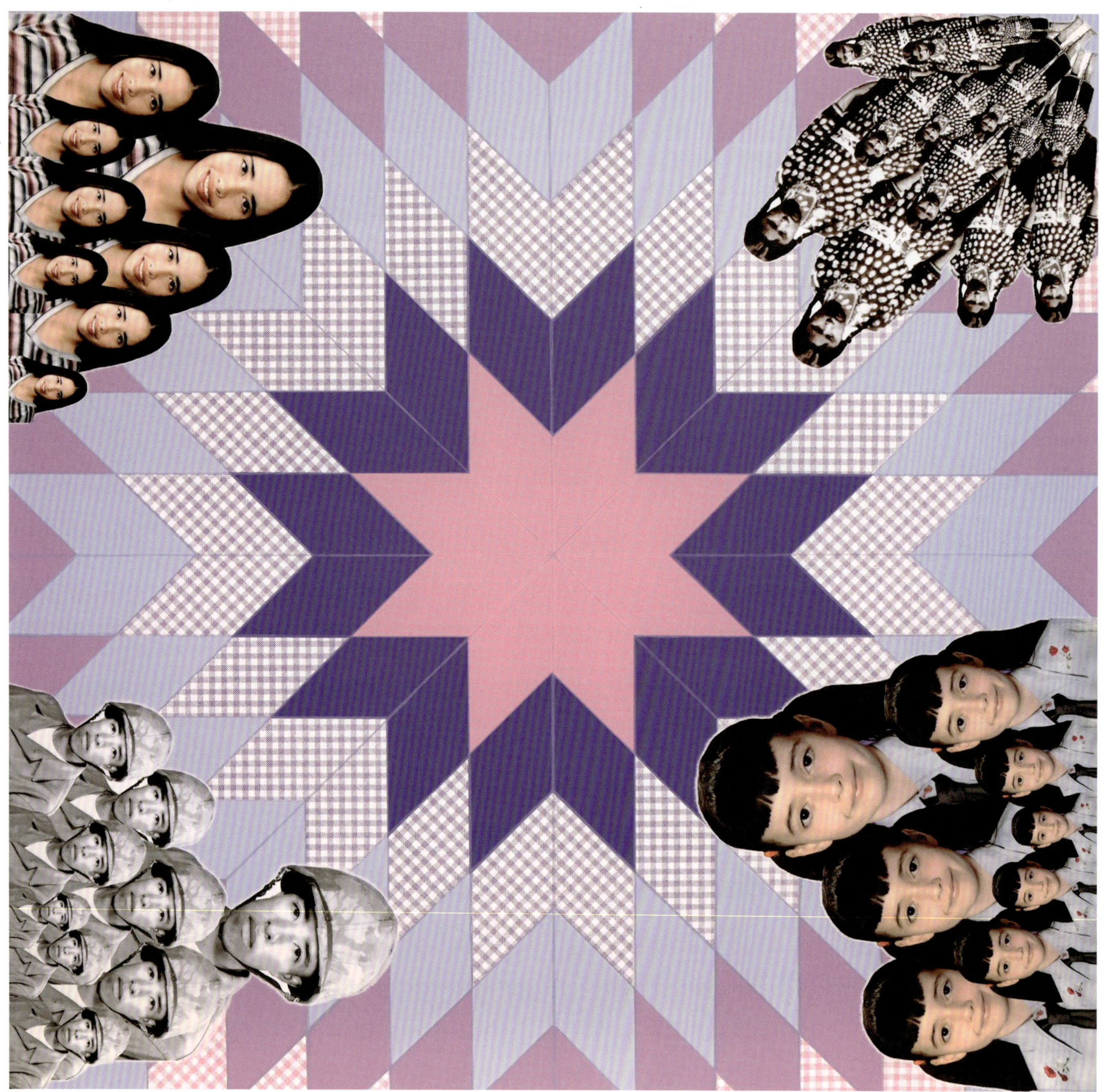

Four Generations

2021

Six-color lithograph on Somerset Satin
white, with archival pigment printed
chine collé on mulberry paper, edition
15 of 16

30.25 x 30 in. (76.8 x 76.2 cm)

Image courtesy of the artist and
Sargent's Daughters © Wendy Red Star

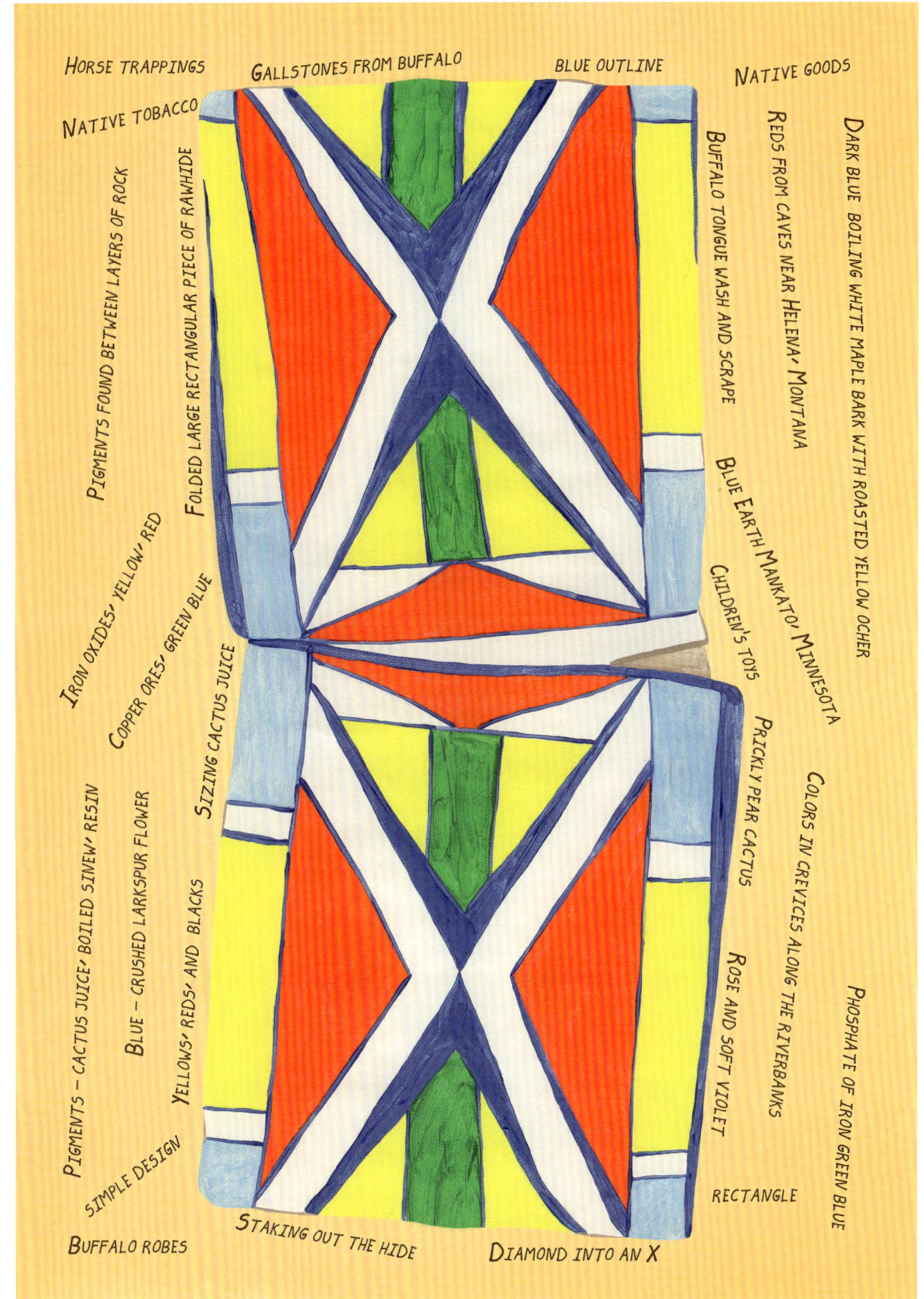

Set C: Shows Going

2023

Archival pigment print on German etching paper, edition 2 of 5

34.5 x 24 in. (87.63 x 60.96 cm)

Image courtesy of the artist and Sargent's Daughters © Wendy Red Star

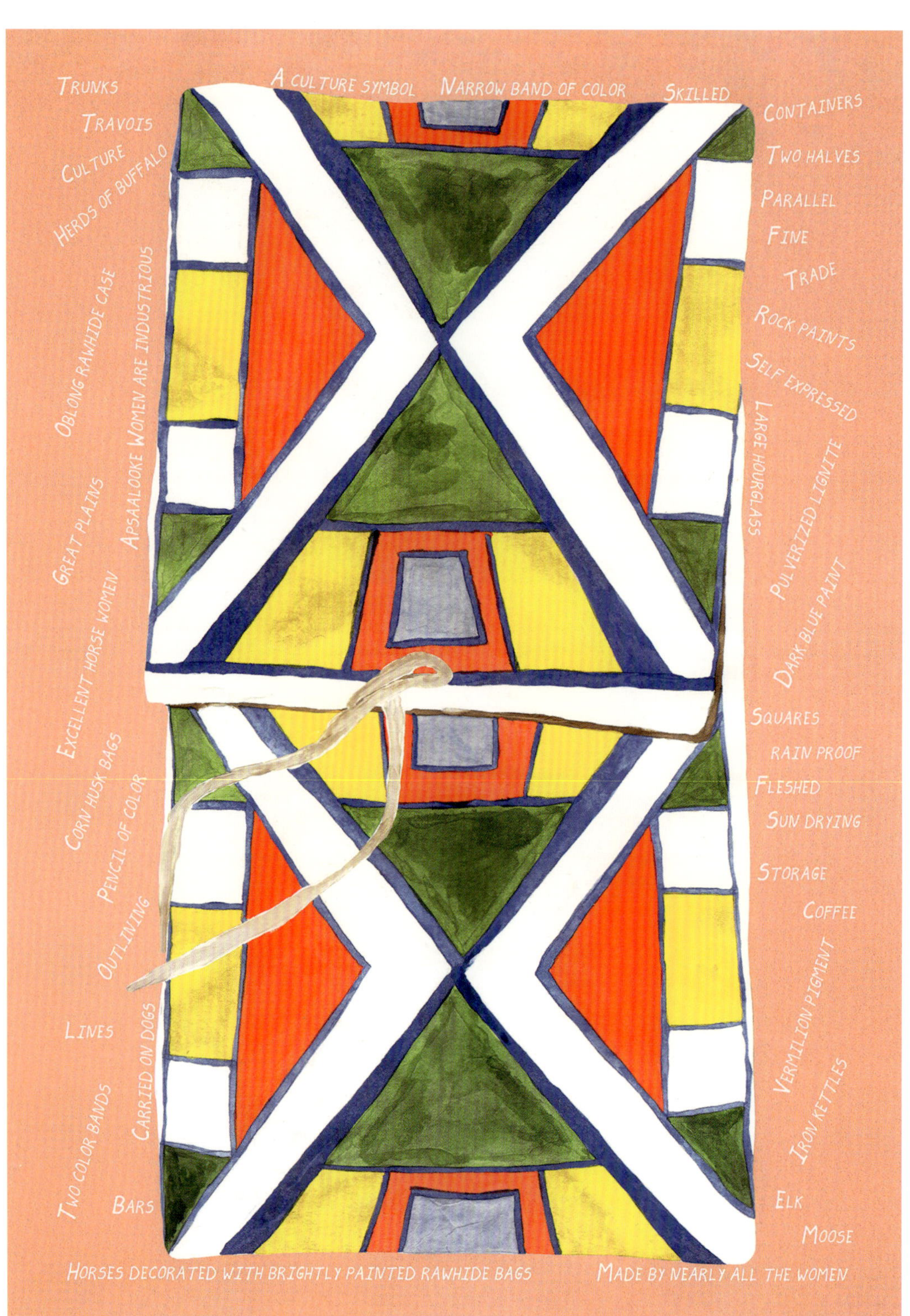

Set C: Buffalo Woman

2023

Archival pigment print on German etching paper, edition 2 of 5

34.5 x 24 in. (87.63 x 60.96 cm)

Image courtesy of the artist and Sargent's Daughters © Wendy Red Star

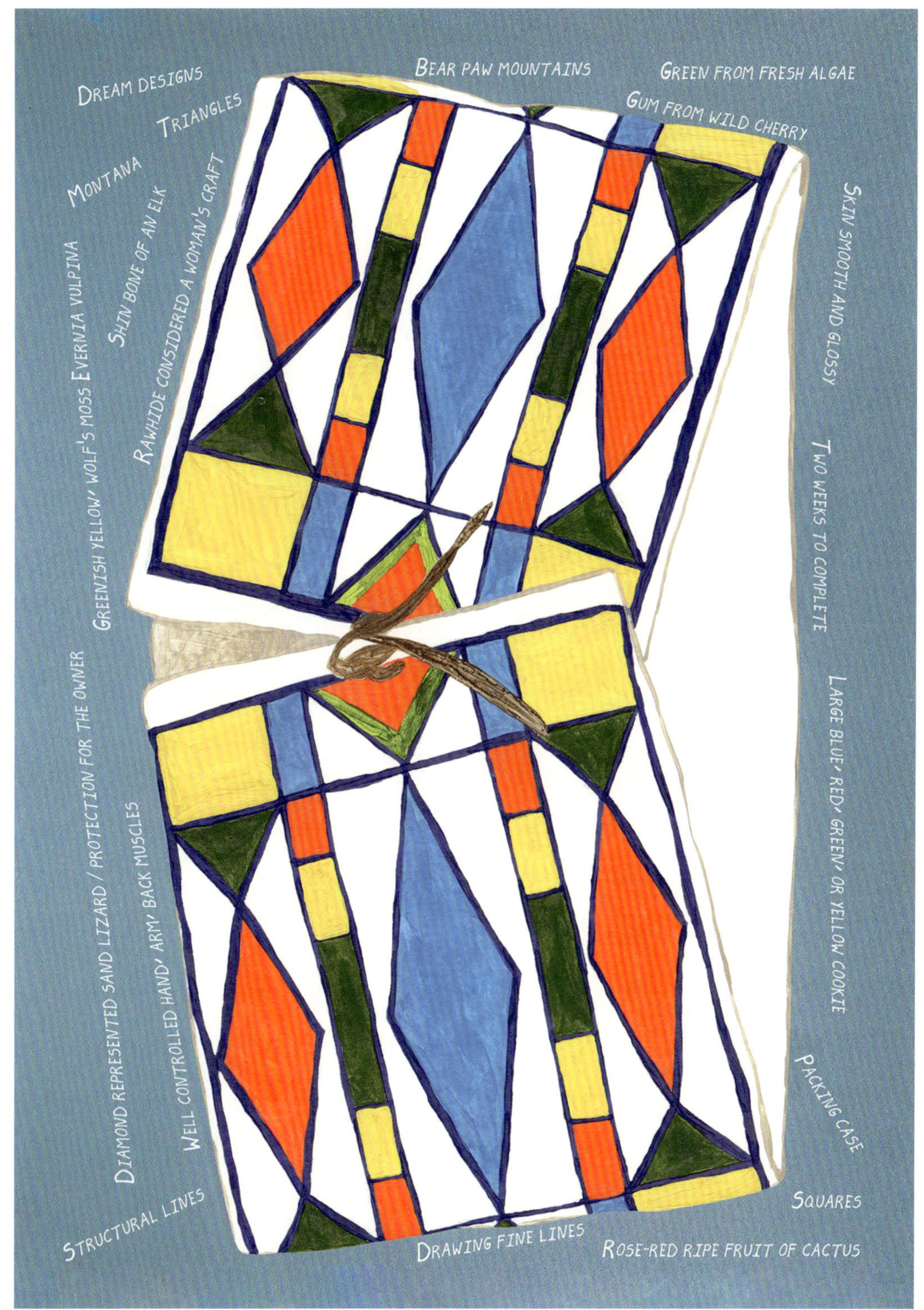

Set A: Brings Things Herself

2023

Archival pigment print, edition 1 of 5

34.5 x 24 in. (87.63 x 60.96 cm)

Image courtesy of the artist and
Sargent's Daughters © Wendy Red Star

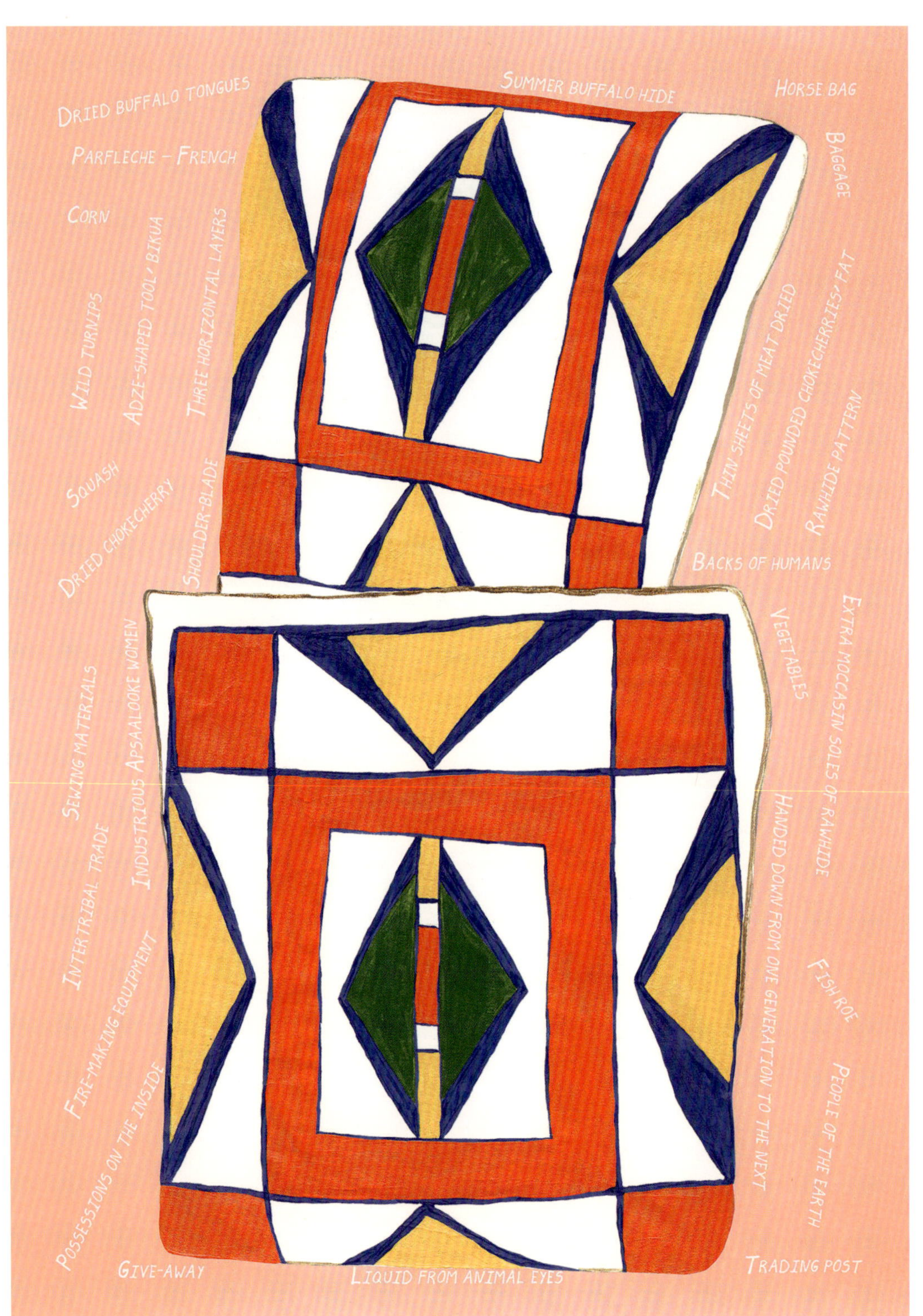

Set A: Ties Up Her Bundles
2023
Archival pigment print, edition 1 of 5
34.5 x 24 in. (87.63 x 60.96 cm)
Image courtesy of the artist and
Sargent's Daughters © Wendy Red Star

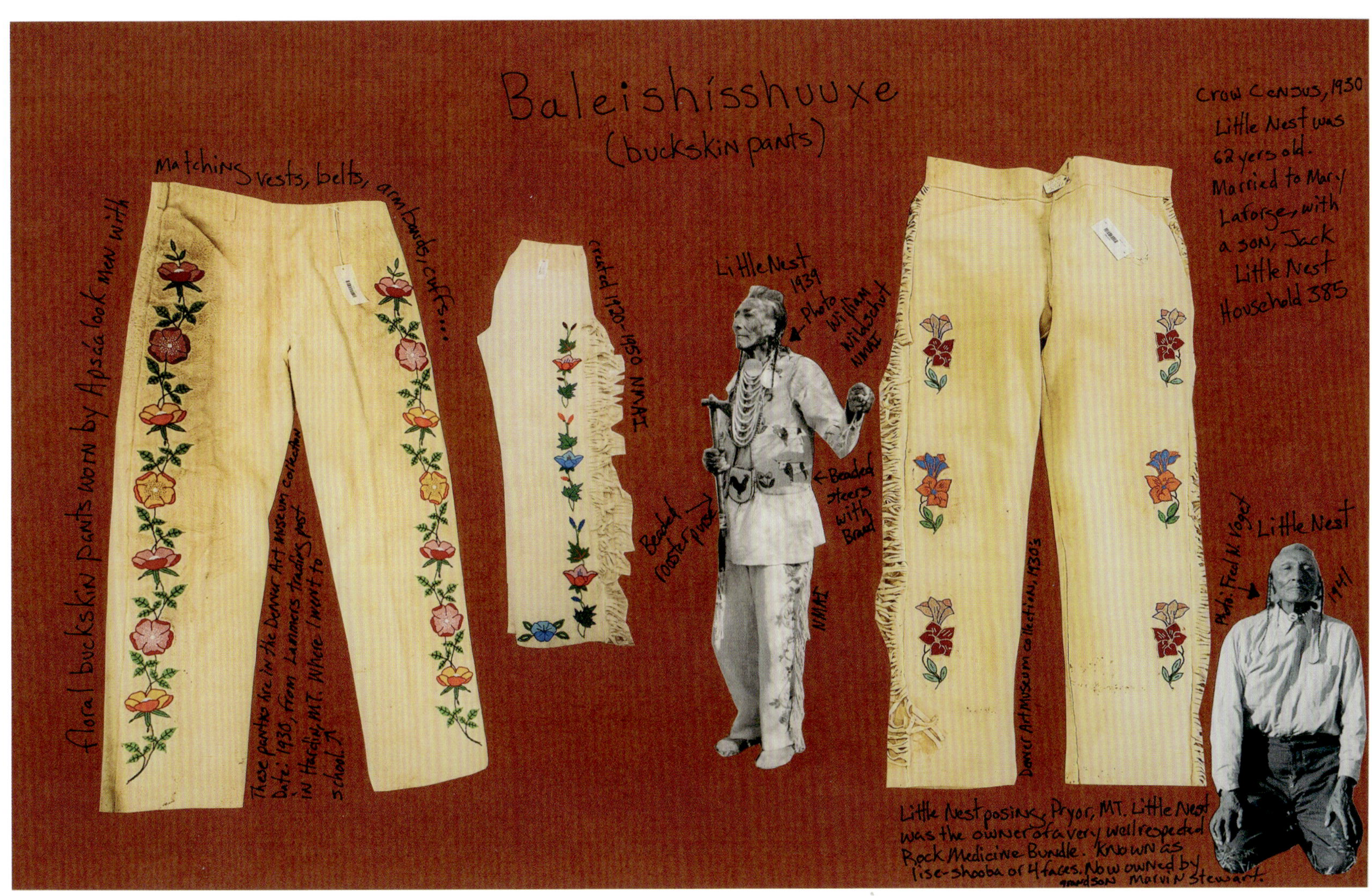

Set E: baleishísshuuxe (buckskin pants)

2023

Archival pigment print on Satin Photo Rag, edition 1 of 3

16 x 25 in. (40.6 x 63.5 cm)

Image courtesy of the artist and Sargent's Daughters © Wendy Red Star

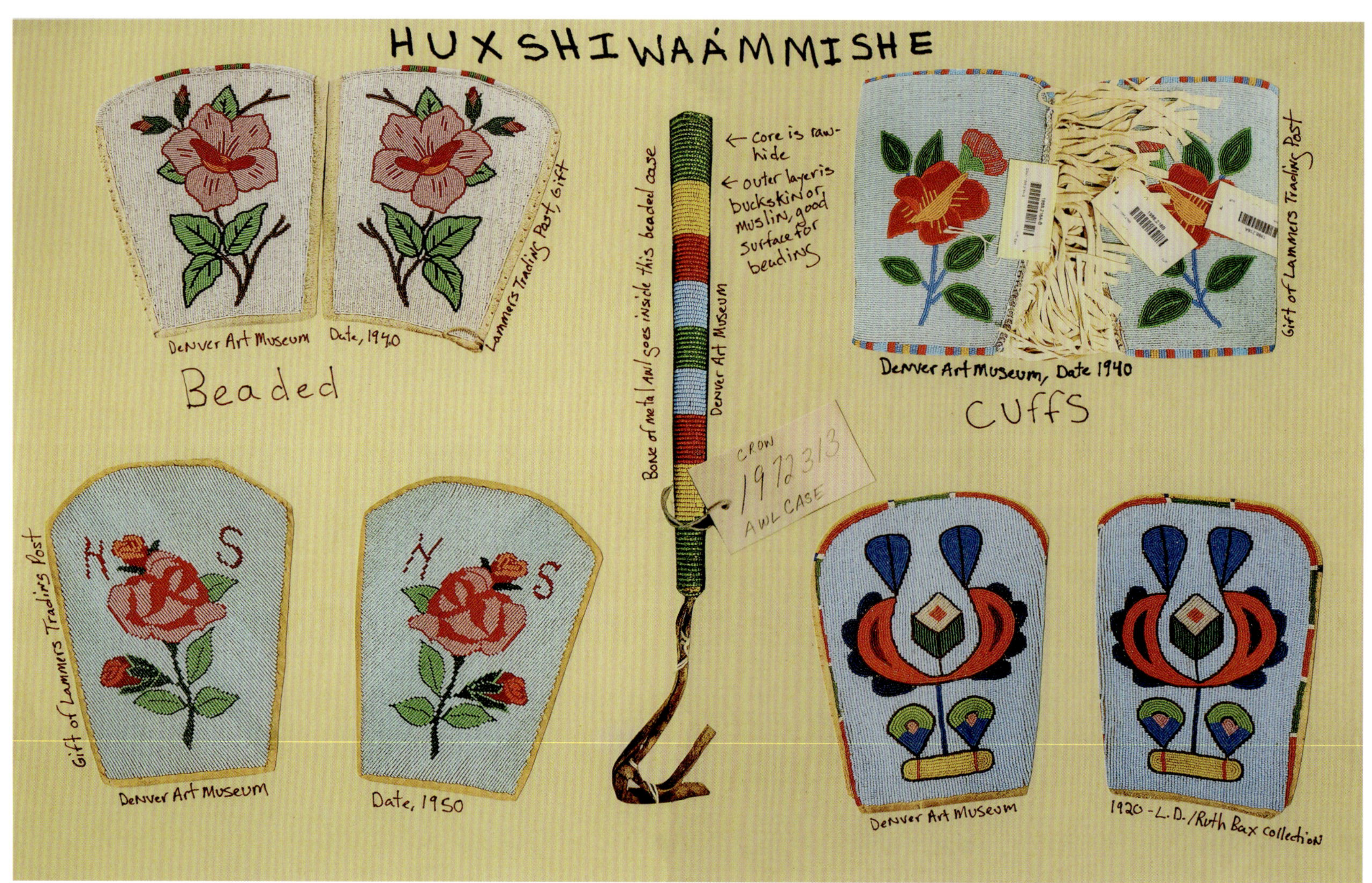

Set E: huxshiwaámmishe (beaded cuffs)

2023

Archival pigment print on Satin Photo Rag, edition 1 of 3

16 x 25 in. (40.6 x 63.5 cm)

Image courtesy of the artist and Sargent's Daughters © Wendy Red Star

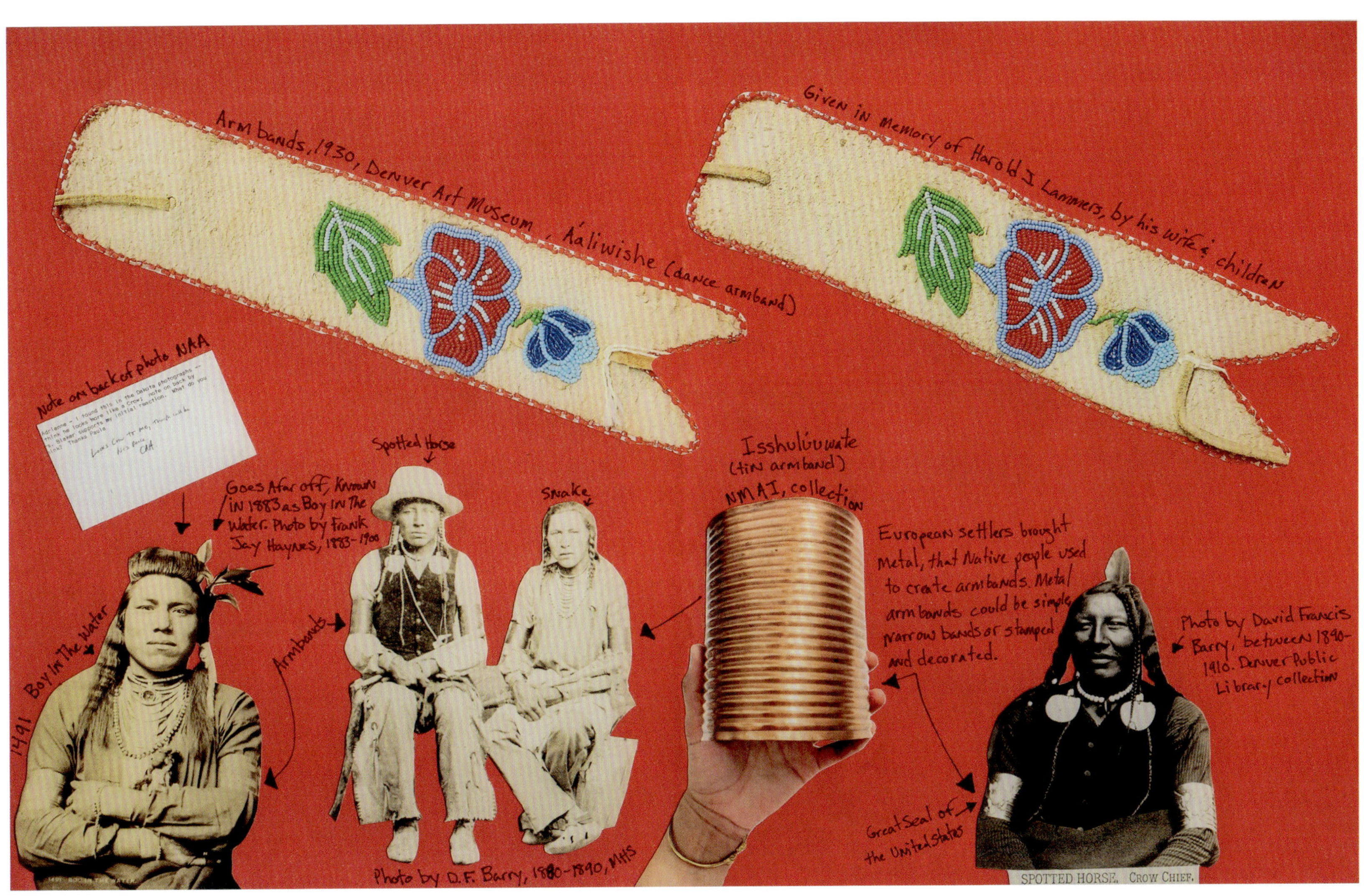

Set E: isshulúuwate (tin armband)

2023

Archival pigment print on Satin Photo
Rag, edition 1 of 3

16 x 25 in. (40.6 x 63.5 cm)

Image courtesy of the artist and
Sargent's Daughters © Wendy Red Star

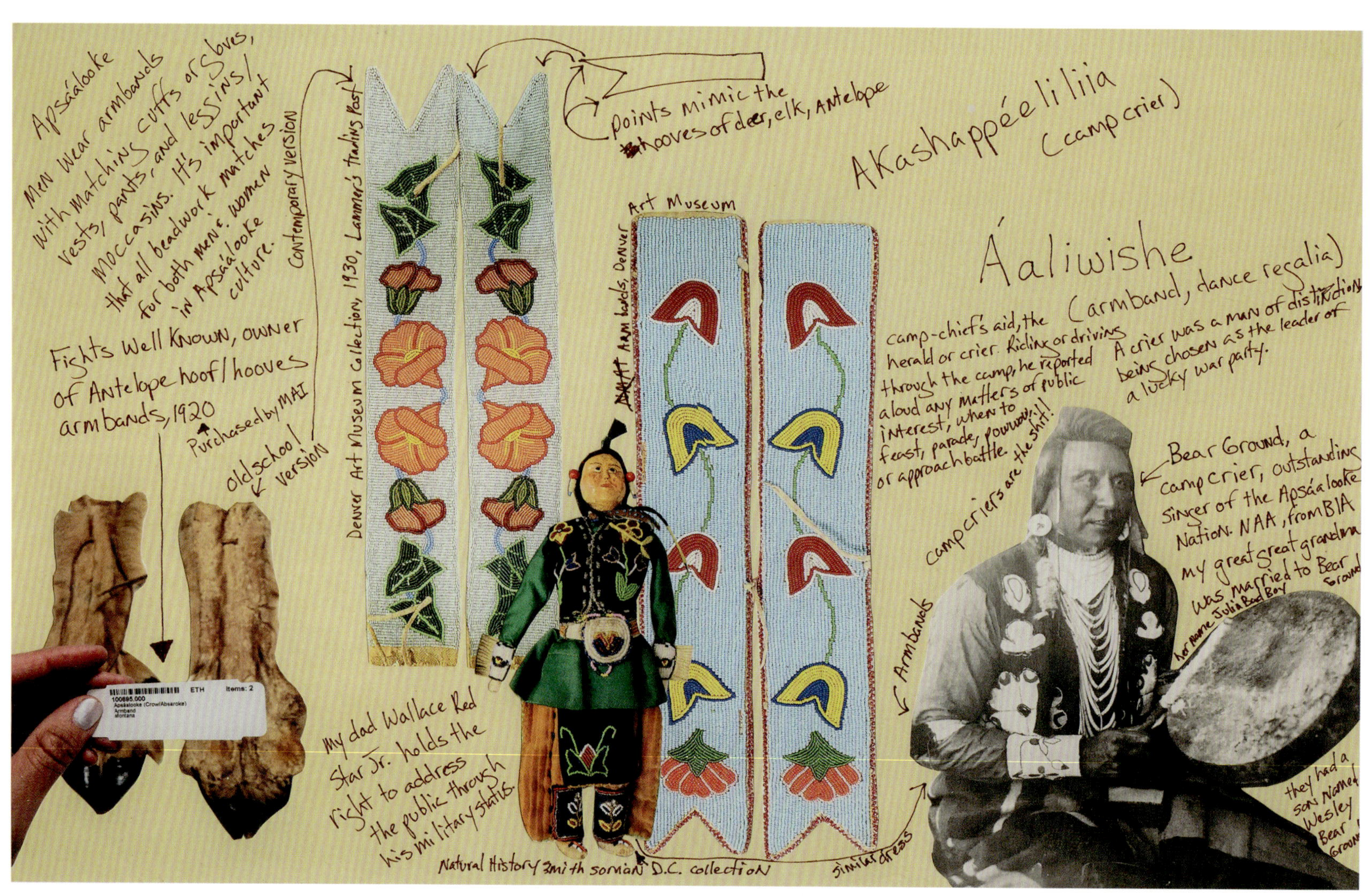

Set E: akashappéeliliia (camp crier)

2023

Archival pigment print on Satin Photo Rag, edition 1 of 3

16 x 25 in. (40.6 x 63.5 cm)

Image courtesy of the artist and Sargent's Daughters © Wendy Red Star

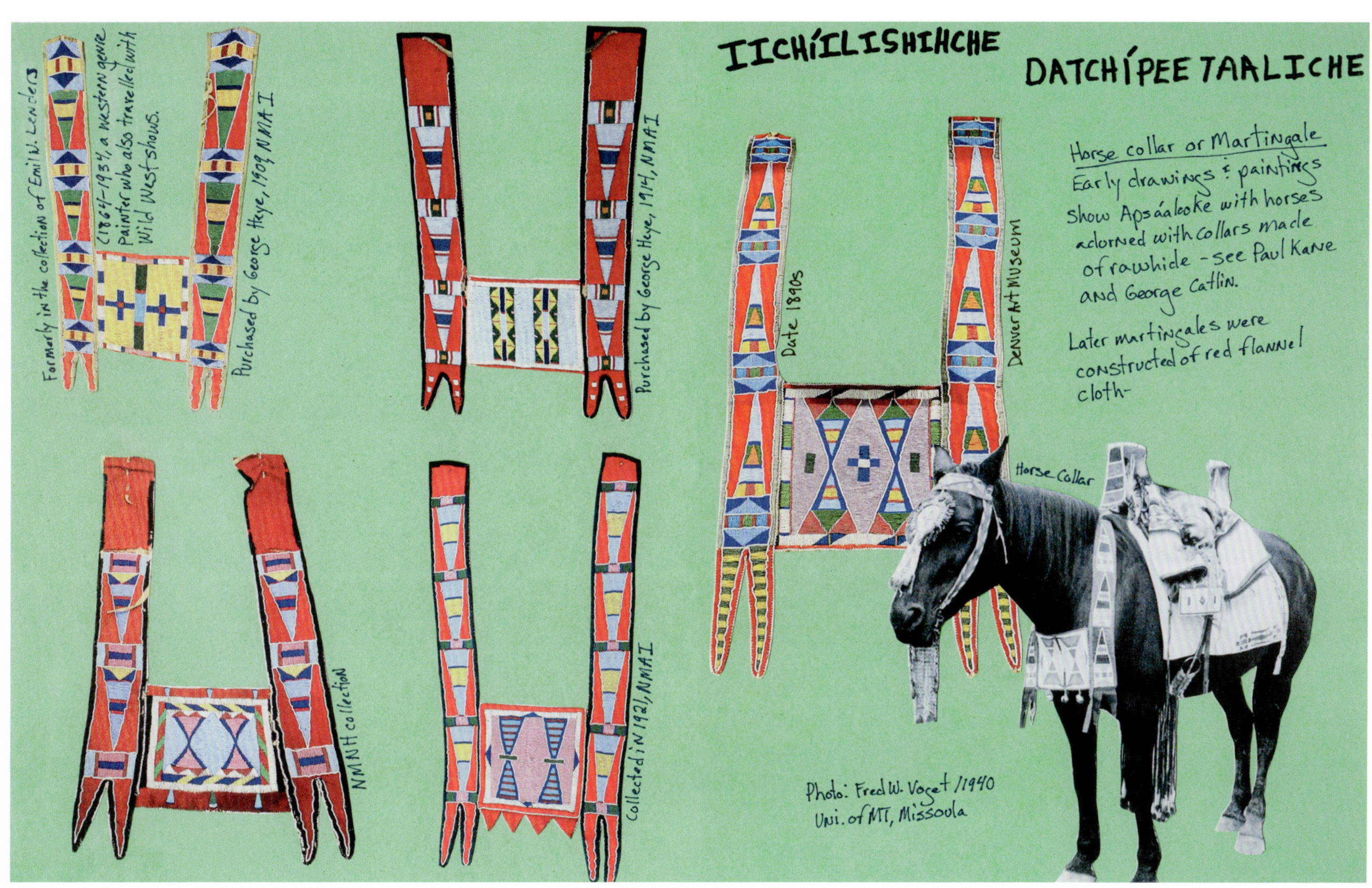

Set F: iichíilishihche
datchípeetaaliche (martingale)

2023

Archival pigment print on Satin Photo Rag, edition 3 of 3

16 x 25 in. (40.6 x 63.5 cm)

Purchase of the Friends of The Trout Gallery, Dickinson College, 2025.19.1

Image courtesy of the artist and Sargent's Daughters © Wendy Red Star

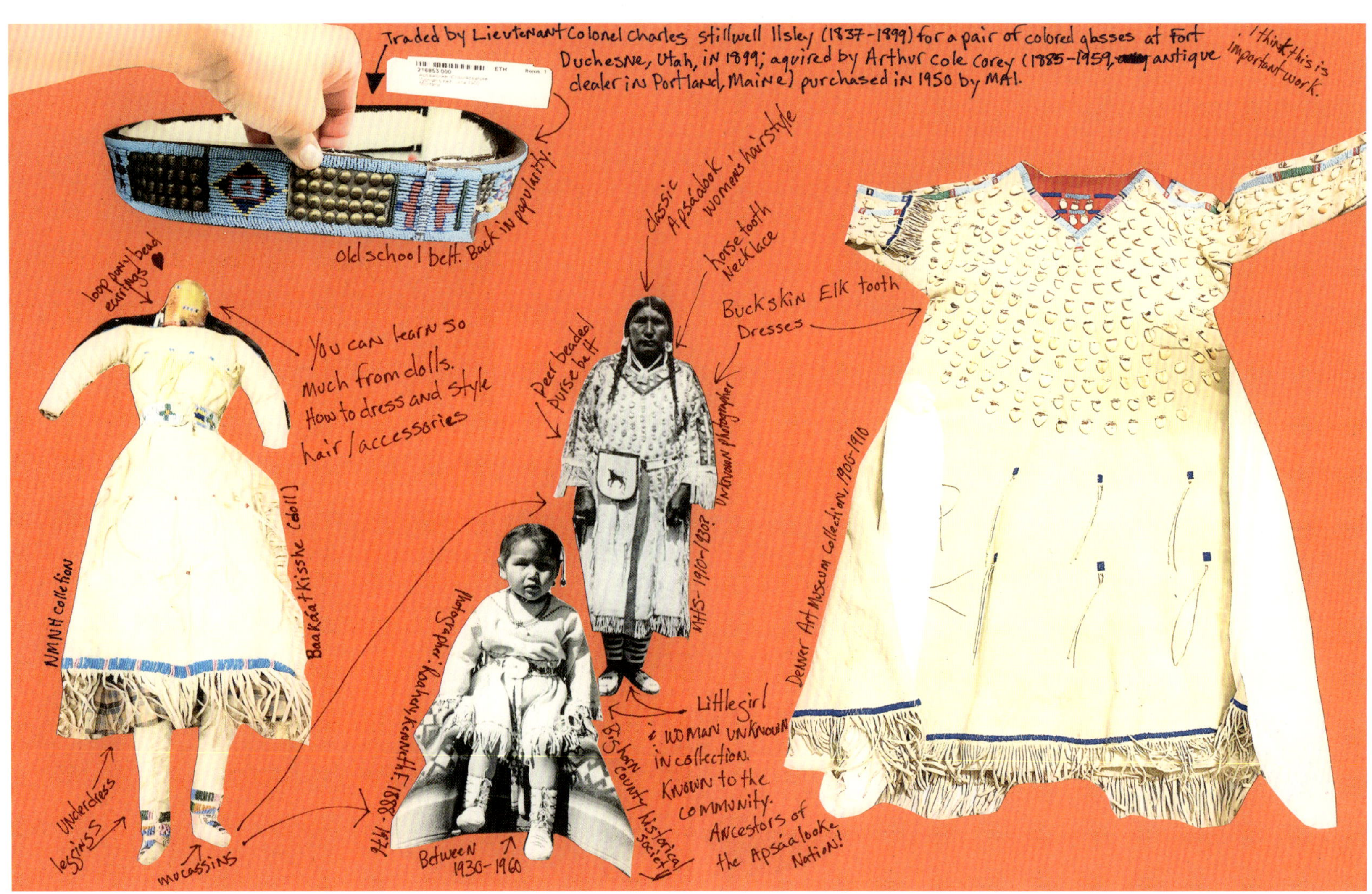

Set F: iíttaashteeuuxe (buckskin dress)

2023

Archival pigment print on Satin Photo Rag, edition 3 of 3

16 x 25 in. (40.6 x 63.5 cm)

Purchase of the Friends of The Trout Gallery, Dickinson College, 2025.19.2

Image courtesy of the artist and Sargent's Daughters © Wendy Red Star

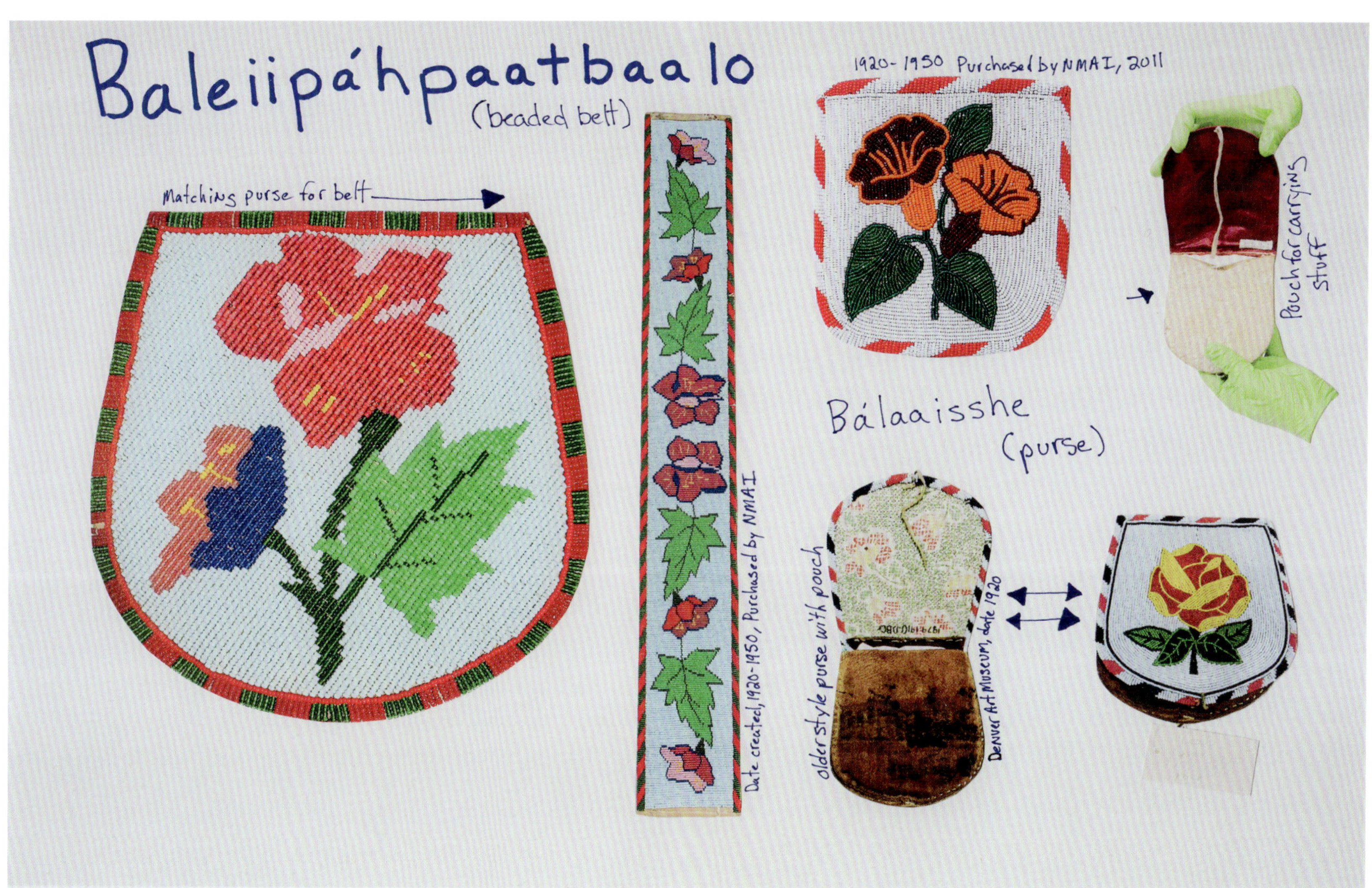

Set F: baleiipáhpaatbaalo (beaded belt) and bálaaisshe (purse)

2023

Archival pigment print on Satin Photo Rag, edition 3 of 3

16 x 25 in. (40.6 x 63.5 cm)

Purchase of the Friends of The Trout Gallery, Dickinson College, 2025.19.3

Image courtesy of the artist and Sargent's Daughters © Wendy Red Star

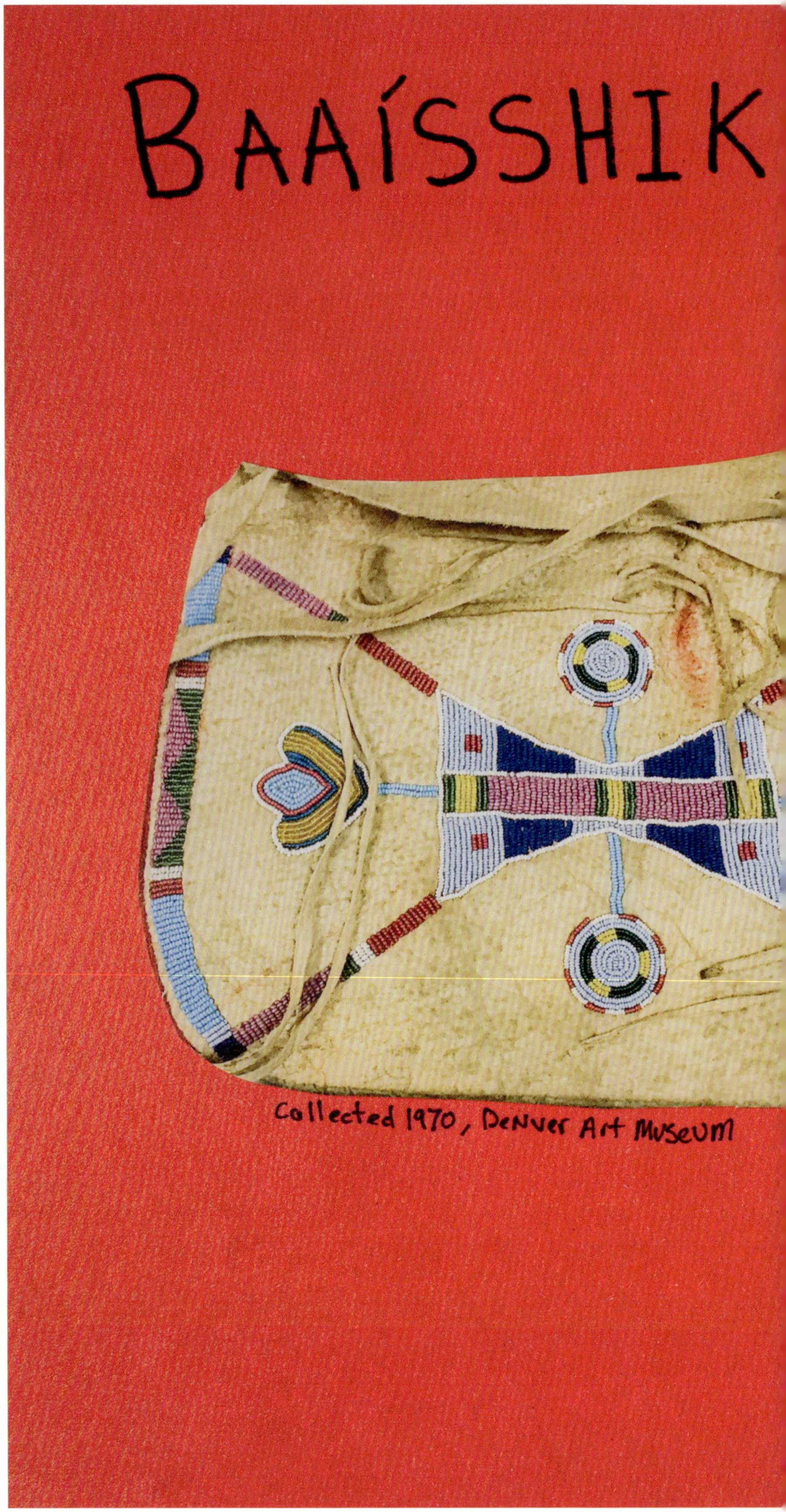

Set F: baaísshikshe (saddle bag)

2023

Archival pigment print on Satin Photo
Rag, edition 3 of 3

16 x 25 in. (40.6 x 63.5 cm)

Purchase of the Friends of The Trout
Gallery, Dickinson College, 2025.19.4

Image courtesy of the artist and
Sargent's Daughters © Wendy Red Star

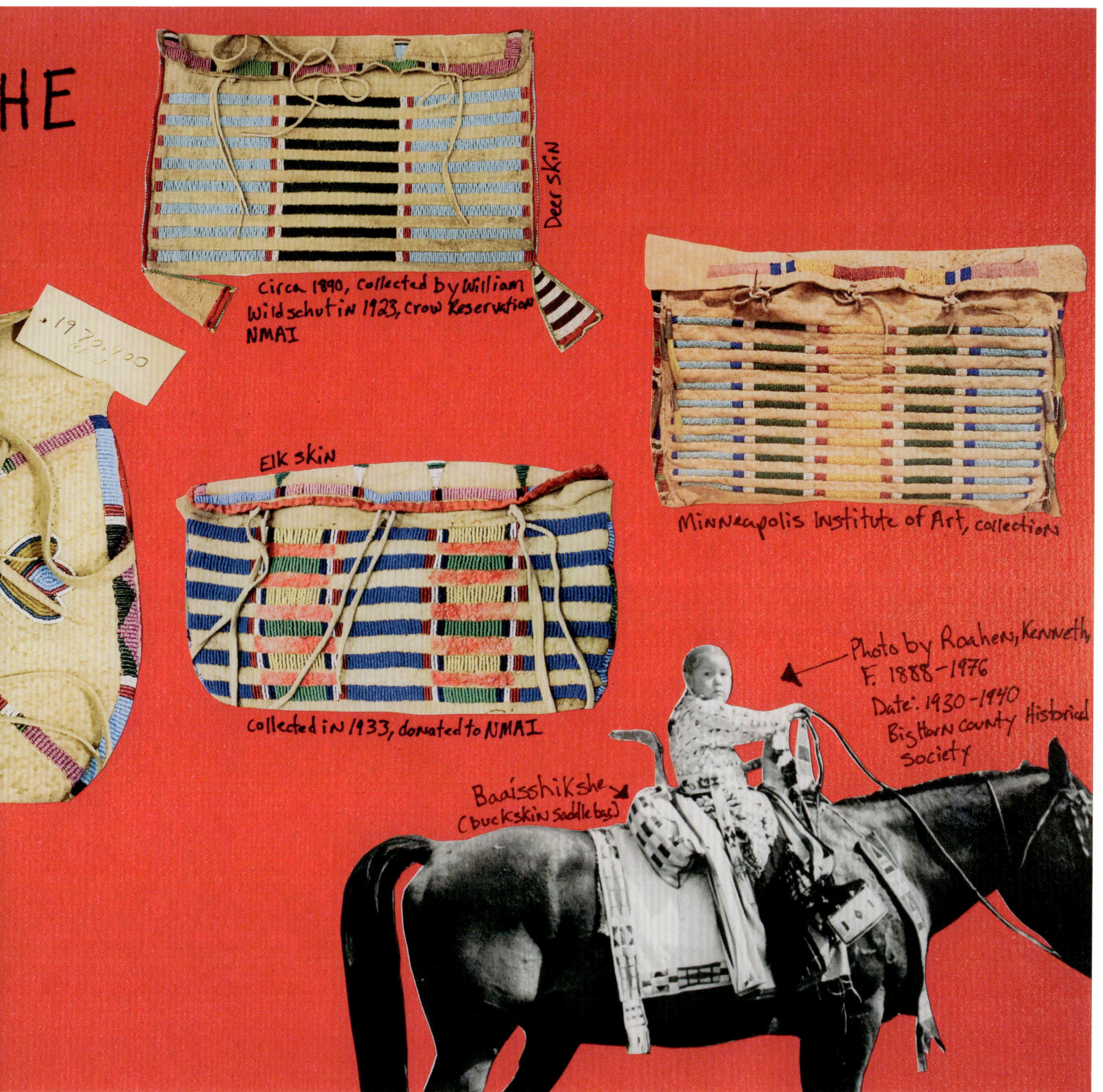
Deer skin
Circa 1890, collected by William Wildschut in 1923, Crow Reservation NMAI
.1970.900
Elk skin
Collected in 1933, donated to NMAI
Minneapolis Institute of Art, collection
Baaisshikshe (buckskin saddle bag)
Photo by Roahen, Kenneth F. 1888-1976
Date: 1930-1940
Big Horn County Historical Society

CHECKLIST OF THE EXHIBITION

The Last Thanks
2006
Archival pigment print
24 x 36 in. (61 x 91.4 cm)
Courtesy Forge Project Collection,
traditional lands of the Moh-He-Con-Nuck
Image courtesy of the artist and Sargent's
Daughters © Wendy Red Star

My Home is Where My Tipi Sits (Sweat Lodges)
2011
Archival pigment print
57 x 72 in. (144.78 x 182.88 cm)
Courtesy Forge Project Collection, traditional lands
of the Moh-He-Con-Nuck
© Wendy Red Star

The Maniacs
2018
Lithograph and screenprint
27 x 19 in. (68.58 x 48.26 cm)
Image courtesy of the artist and Sargent's
Daughters © Wendy Red Star

Catalogue Number 1949.72
2019
Pigment print on archival paper, edition 1 of 10 and
2 AP
28 x 18 in. (71.1 x 45.7 cm)
Image courtesy of the artist and Sargent's
Daughters © Wendy Red Star

Catalogue Number 1938.52
2019
Pigment print on archival paper, edition 1 of 10 and
2 AP
28 x 18 in. (71.1 x 45.7 cm)
Image courtesy of the artist and Sargent's
Daughters © Wendy Red Star

Catalogue Number 1941.30.1
2019
Pigment print on archival paper, edition 1 of 10 and
2 AP
28 x 18 in. (71.1 x 45.7 cm)
Image courtesy of the artist and Sargent's
Daughters© Wendy Red Star

Catalogue Number 1946.82.1
2019
Pigment print on archival paper, edition 1 of 10 and
2 AP
28 x 18 in. (71.1 x 45.7 cm)
Image courtesy of the artist and Sargent's
Daughters © Wendy Red Star

Catalogue Number 1949.66
2019
Pigment print on archival paper, edition 1 of 10 and
2 AP
28 x 18 in. (71.1 x 45.7 cm)
Image courtesy of the artist and Sargent's
Daughters © Wendy Red Star

Catalogue Number 1949.73
2019
Pigment print on archival paper, edition 1 of 10 and
2 AP
28 x 18 in. (71.1 x 45.7 cm)
Image courtesy of the artist and Sargent's
Daughters © Wendy Red Star

Catalogue Number 1948.102
2019
Pigment print on archival paper, edition 1 of 10 and
2 AP
18 x 28 in. (45.7 cm x 71.1 cm)
Image courtesy of the artist and Sargent's
Daughters © Wendy Red Star

Catalogue Number 1950.74
2019
Pigment print on archival paper, edition 1 of 10 and
2 AP
18 x 28 in. (45.7 cm x 71.1 cm)
Image courtesy of the artist and Sargent's
Daughters © Wendy Red Star

Catalogue Number 1935.33.a,b.
2019
Pigment print on archival paper, edition 1 of 10 and
2 AP
18 x 28 in. (45.7 cm x 71.1 cm)
Image courtesy of the artist and Sargent's
Daughters © Wendy Red Star

Catalogue Number 1944.26
2019
Pigment print on archival paper, edition 1 of 10 and
2 AP
18 x 28 in. (45.7 cm x 71.1 cm)
Image courtesy of the artist and Sargent's
Daughters © Wendy Red Star

Catalogue Number 1947.110
2019
Pigment print on archival paper, edition 1 of 10 and
2 AP
18 x 28 in. (45.7 cm x 71.1 cm)
Image courtesy of the artist and Sargent's
Daughters © Wendy Red Star

Catalogue Number 1949.105
2019
Pigment print on archival paper, edition 1 of 10 and
2 AP
18 x 28 in. (45.7 cm x 71.1 cm)
Image courtesy of the artist and Sargent's
Daughters © Wendy Red Star

Catalogue Number 1949.67.a,b.
2019
Pigment print on archival paper, edition 1 of 10 and
2 AP
28 x 18 in. (71.1 x 45.7 cm)
Image courtesy of the artist and Sargent's
Daughters © Wendy Red Star

Catalogue Number 1950.76
2019
Pigment print on archival paper, edition 1 of 10 and
2 AP, 28 x 18 in. (71.1 x 45.7 cm)
Image courtesy of the artist and Sargent's
Daughters © Wendy Red Star

Dust
2021
Three-color lithograph on Somerset Satin soft
white, with archival pigment printed chine collé on
mulberry paper, edition 15 of 25
20.25 x 20 in. (51.44 x 50.8 cm)
Image courtesy of the artist and Sargent's
Daughters © Wendy Red Star

Her Dreams Are True (Julia Bad Boy)
2021

Six-color lithograph on Somerset Satin soft white, with archival pigment printed chine collé on mulberry paper, edition 15 of 25

20.25 x 20 in. (51.44 x 50.8 cm)

Image courtesy of the artist and Sargent's Daughters © Wendy Red Star

––––––––––

Four Generations
2021

Six-color lithograph on Somerset Satin white, with archival pigment printed chine collé on mulberry paper, edition 15 of 16

30.25 x 30 in. (76.8 x 76.2 cm)

Image courtesy of the artist and Sargent's Daughters © Wendy Red Star

––––––––––

Set C: Shows Going
2023

Archival pigment print on German etching paper, edition 2 of 5

34.5 x 24 in. (87.63 x 60.96 cm)

Image courtesy of the artist and Sargent's Daughters © Wendy Red Star

––––––––––

Set C: Buffalo Woman
2023

Archival pigment print on German etching paper, edition 2 of 5

34.5 x 24 in. (87.63 x 60.96 cm)

Image courtesy of the artist and Sargent's Daughters © Wendy Red Star

––––––––––

Set A: Brings Things Herself
2023

Archival pigment print, edition 1 of 5

34.5 x 24 in. (87.63 x 60.96 cm)

Image courtesy of the artist and Sargent's Daughters © Wendy Red Star

––––––––––

Set A: Ties Up Her Bundles
2023

Archival pigment print, edition 1 of 5

34.5 x 24 in. (87.63 x 60.96 cm)

Image courtesy of the artist and Sargent's Daughters © Wendy Red Star

––––––––––

Set E: baleishísshuuxe (buckskin pants)
2023

Archival pigment print on Satin Photo Rag, edition 1 of 3

16 x 25 in. (40.6 x 63.5 cm)

Image courtesy of the artist and Sargent's Daughters © Wendy Red Star

––––––––––

Set E: huxshiwaámmishe (beaded cuffs)
2023

Archival pigment print on Satin Photo Rag, edition 1 of 3

16 x 25 in. (40.6 x 63.5 cm)

Image courtesy of the artist and Sargent's Daughters © Wendy Red Star

––––––––––

Set E: isshulúuwate (tin armband)
2023

Archival pigment print on Satin Photo Rag, edition 1 of 3

16 x 25 in. (40.6 x 63.5 cm)

Image courtesy of the artist and Sargent's Daughters © Wendy Red Star

––––––––––

Set E: akashappéeliliia (camp crier)
2023

Archival pigment print on Satin Photo Rag, edition 1 of 3

16 x 25 in. (40.6 x 63.5 cm)

Image courtesy of the artist and Sargent's Daughters © Wendy Red Star

––––––––––

Set F: iichíilishihche datchípeetaaliche (martingale)
2023

Archival pigment print on Satin Photo Rag, edition 3 of 3

16 x 25 in. (40.6 x 63.5 cm)

Purchase of the Friends of The Trout Gallery, Dickinson College, 2025.19.1

Image courtesy of the artist and Sargent's Daughters © Wendy Red Star

––––––––––

Set F: iíttaashteeuuxe (buckskin dress)
2023

Archival pigment print on Satin Photo Rag, edition 3 of 3

16 x 25 in. (40.6 x 63.5 cm)

Purchase of the Friends of The Trout Gallery, Dickinson College, 2025.19.2

Image courtesy of the artist and Sargent's Daughters © Wendy Red Star

––––––––––

Set F: baleiipáhpaatbaalo (beaded belt) and bálaaisshe (purse)
2023

Archival pigment print on Satin Photo Rag, edition 3 of 3

16 x 25 in. (40.6 x 63.5 cm)

Purchase of the Friends of The Trout Gallery, Dickinson College, 2025.19.3

Image courtesy of the artist and Sargent's Daughters © Wendy Red Star

––––––––––

Set F: baaísshikshe (saddle bag)
2023

Archival pigment print on Satin Photo Rag, edition 3 of 3

16 x 25 in. (40.6 x 63.5 cm)

Purchase of the Friends of The Trout Gallery, Dickinson College, 2025.19.4

Image courtesy of the artist and Sargent's Daughters © Wendy Red Star

––––––––––

CONTRIBUTORS

WENDY RED STAR

Wendy Red Star (b.1981, Billings, MT) lives and works in Portland, OR. An enrolled member of the Apsáalooke (Crow) Tribe, Red Star works across disciplines to explore the intersections of Native American ideologies and colonialist structures, both historically and in contemporary society.

Red Star has exhibited in the United States and abroad at venues including the Metropolitan Museum of Art (New York, NY); The Newark Museum (Newark, NJ), Brooklyn Museum (Brooklyn, NY), The Broad (Los Angeles, CA); the Getty Museum (Los Angeles, CA); Fondation Cartier pour l'Art Contemporain (Paris, France); Seattle Art Museum (Seattle, WA); Portland Art Museum (Portland, OR); the Museum of Contemporary Art Chicago (Chicago, IL); St. Louis Art Museum (St. Louis, MO), among many others. Her monumental sculpture, *The Soil You See...*, was included in *Beyond Granite: Pulling Together*, the first curated outdoor exhibition in the history of the National Mall (Washington, D.C), organized by Monument Lab in 2023. The work was then acquired by Tippet Rise Art Center (Fishtail, MT).

Her work is in over 60 public collections, including the Museum of Modern Art (New York, NY); the Whitney Museum of American Art (New York, NY); the Guggenheim Museum (New York, NY); the Amon Carter Museum of American Art (Fort Worth, TX); the Denver Art Museum (Denver, CO); Crystal Bridges Museum of American Art (Bentonville, AK); the Baltimore Museum of Art (Baltimore, MD); the Fralin Museum of Art at the University of Virginia (Charlottesville, VA); the Nasher Museum of Art at Duke University (Durham, NC); the Williams College Museum of Art (Williamstown, MA); San Antonio Museum of Art (San Antonio, TX); and the British Museum (London, UK), among others.

Red Star holds a BFA from Montana State University, Bozeman, and an MFA in sculpture from University of California, Los Angeles. She served as visiting lecturer at institutions including Yale University (New Haven, CT), the Banff Centre (Banff, Canada), National Gallery of Victoria in Melbourne (Melbourne, Australia), Dartmouth College (Hanover, NH), and CalArts (Valencia, CA). In 2017, Red Star was awarded the Louis Comfort Tiffany Award, and in 2018 she received a Smithsonian Artist Research Fellowship. In 2022, Red Star was an Anonymous Was A Woman Grant recipient. Red Star was named a 2024 MacArthur Fellow.

She is represented by Sargent's Daughters in New York, NY and Roberts Projects in Los Angeles, CA.

LAURA M. FURLAN

Laura M. Furlan is Associate Professor of English at the University of Massachusetts Amherst, where she teaches courses in Native American literature, American Studies, and creative nonfiction. She earned a PhD in English from the University of California, Santa Barbara. She is the author of *Indigenous Cities: Urban Indian Fiction and the Histories of Relocation* (2017, Nebraska), a study of contemporary Indigenous novels that are set in urban spaces. In 2020, she co-edited a special issue of the *Massachusetts Review* of new Native writing, and in 2021 she co-edited a special issue of *Studies in American Indian Literatures* focused on Deborah Miranda's memoir *Bad Indians* in which her award-winning essay, "The Archives of Deborah Miranda's *Bad Indians*" appears. She is working on a book project that studies archival remediation in contemporary Native writing and art. She also publishes creative nonfiction about her experience as an adoptee of Native descent. She is the current president of the Association for the Study of American Indian Literatures (ASAIL).

DARREN EDWARD LONE FIGHT

Darren Edward Lone Fight, an enrolled member of the Three Affiliated Tribes (Mandan, Hidatsa, Sahnish) and citizen Mvskoke Creek (Natchez Nation), is a scholar and educator whose interdisciplinary work merges Indigenous ontologies, aesthetics, and futurism. He was instrumental in envisioning and establishing the Center for the Futures of Native Peoples (CFNP) at Dickinson College, helping secure major philanthropic support before serving as its inaugural, interim executive director. Today the CFNP helps facilitate connections between tribal nations, Indigenous intellectuals and artists, boarding school descendants and scholars, and Dickinson's own community while advancing critical dialogues around the legacy of Indian boarding schools.

Dr. Lone Fight earned his BA in Philosophy and Religion from the University of North Dakota and completed his MA and PhD in American Studies at the University of Massachusetts Amherst. He contributed to the formation of Tufts University's Native American and Indigenous Studies minor as visiting faculty before joining Dickinson College as a faculty member in American Studies in 2020. His work focuses on transforming sites and stories of historical trauma into spaces of Indigenous possibility, survivance, and resurgence. Nationally, he has shared insights on platforms such as CBC, WGBH, and WITF's "The Spark," discussing everything from Indigenous influences in *Star Wars* and Native American flags/sports mascots to the Carlisle Indian Industrial School's challenging legacy. Through these dialogues, he seeks to amplify and center Indigenous perspectives about the future of scholarship, culture, and art, forging new pathways for Indigenous intellectual sovereignty and bridging communities across time and place.

SHANNON EGAN

Shannon Egan is the Director of The Trout Gallery, the Art Museum of Dickinson College, where she curates exhibitions and also teaches courses in art history and museum studies. Prior to her arrival at Dickinson, Egan served as the Director of the Schmucker Art Gallery at Gettysburg College for 16 years. Egan received her MA and PhD in the History of Art from Johns Hopkins University and her BA from the University of North Carolina at Chapel Hill. Egan is the author of articles on photographers Edward S. Curtis and Jeff Wall and has curated, coordinated, and published catalogues for numerous exhibitions, including solo exhibitions of works by artists Kara Walker, Martin Puryear, William Clutz, Glenn Ligon, Michael Scoggins, and Sam Van Aken, among many others.

With photo-historian Marthe Tolnes Fjellestad, Egan is the co-editor of the book *Across the West and Toward the North: Norwegian and American Landscape Photography* (University of Utah Press, 2022) and co-curator of the accompanying exhibition of the same name that traveled to museums throughout the United States and Norway (2021-2024). In support of the exhibition, Egan and Fjellestad were awarded grants from the Wyeth Foundation for American Art, the United Stated Embassy in Oslo, the American-Scandinavian Foundation, and the Fritt Ord Foundation. Fjellestad and Egan are in the process of co-curating a large-scale exhibition examining artists working in the Arctic.

This publication was produced in part through the generous support of the Helen Trout Memorial Fund and the Ruth Trout Endowment at Dickinson College.

Wendy Red Star: Her Dreams Are True was presented at The Trout Gallery, Dickinson College, September 26, 2025 – February 7, 2026.

Published by The Trout Gallery, the Art Museum of Dickinson College
Carlisle, Pennsylvania, 17013
Distributed by D.A.P., Distributed Art Publishers, Inc., New York, 10013

All images by Wendy Red Star © 2025 Wendy Red Star

Publication copyright © 2025 The Trout Gallery. All rights reserved. No part of this publication may be reproduced, stored in a retrieval system, or transmitted, in any form or by any means, electronic, mechanical, photocopying, recording or otherwise, without written permission from The Trout Gallery.

Editor: Shannon Egan, PhD
Design: Ayumi Yasuda
Printing: Brilliant, Exton, Pennsylvania

ISBN: 979-8-9869735-4-8

Printed in the United States

Wendy Red Star is represented by Sargent's Daughters, New York.

———————

Cover image:
Set F: iíttaashteeuuxe (buckskin dress)
2023
Archival pigment print on Satin Photo Rag, edition 3 of 3
16 x 25 in. (40.6 x 63.5 cm)
Purchase of the Friends of The Trout Gallery, Dickinson College, 2025.19.2
Image courtesy of the artist and Sargent's Daughters © Wendy Red Star